# WE'RE ALMOST THERE

RABBI DOVID M. COHEN

# WE'RE ALMOST THERE

→ LIVING WITH PATIENCE, PERSEVERANCE & PURPOSE ←

COMMUNITY   LIFE & DEATH   INSPIRATION

RAISING CHILDREN EXCEPTIONAL NEEDS

SHIDD

MARITAL HARMONY

MOSAICA PRESS

Mosaica Press, Inc.

© 2016 by Mosaica Press

Interior Design by Daniella Kirsch

Typeset by Rayzel Broyde

Published and distributed by:

Mosaica Press, Inc.

www.mosaicapress.com

info@mosaicapress.com

In memory of

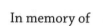

# HaRav Yechezkel ben Leib z"l

In memory of

# Nessie Chana bas Berel Yosef

a wonderful wife, mother and friend to all who
knew her, who was always doing for others.

# YOUNG ISRAEL OF WEST HEMPSTEAD

630 Hempstead Avenue   •   West Hempstead, NY 11552

Rabbi Dovid Cohen's Torah thoughts finely blend ancient chochmah and modern relevance. They possess, like the avnei choshen of his ancestors, illuminating insight. More significantly Reb Dovid's writings are fulfillment of נשא על לב carried in a heart replete with profound love of Torah and the unquenchable desire to be an inspiring teacher of Torah.

Yasher Koach on behalf of a very proud community in West Hempstead.

*Yehuda Kelemer*

Yehuda Kelemer

# ישיבת ברכת מרדכי
## YESHIVA BIRCHAS MORDECHAI

הרב יעקב פרידמן
ראש הישיבה

בס"ד

אלול לפ"ק שנת ישועה קרובה

לכבוד ידי"נ והרה"ג כנפ"י הר' דוד כהן שליט"א

הגיעני אליך לקרובה לשמוע היקר והגדול חלף ונדר
עמנו ואהבתי שוכן אלו חדוה וקהונה, היה לי ברכה
חיבוך והתוסררות מהדברים החשובים ורואין, הרבה ברכה
והכוונה לריסקלית נכונה ולאהבל יפר קריו ואמויך
אמתיך, ואלה לראות קלת עבר אליך בקורה וקירולה
וגרואה הוקית, וכן אז אהליק הראשך ושולתן אמורינו
של רצו אונית ונטינוזיק ברך ואונגא האון ל'
קפלתי וגינקי גרנק הגיול קפבכה להגדל ווד
ונמאינויק הולב, ולהאיק הגדנק הגוע להגודל ולהדרך
עד ד' אהל גלי האולד, לזדן לאחה ונחם להרחב הדצת
ואתן לפני ברכה והכלותה ק"ש

יד"נ
האוה"ר
...ק ברידמן

# TABLE OF CONTENTS

# ACKNOWLEDGMENTS

lthough I have many life ambitions, I never truly contemplated writing a book. Immediately before Pesach 5774, I received an e-mail from Mosaica Press inquiring if I had interest in publishing a book. An interesting idea, I thought to myself. I had done some writing of articles in recent years and was curious what it would actually take to complete a book. After a few discussions with Rabbi Yaacov Haber and Rabbi Doron Kornbluth, I decided to take the plunge. This project has certainly become a labor of love and has possibly sparked some ideas for subsequent projects as well.

I'd like to thank Rabbi Haber and R' Doron for their input and expertise in ensuring that I put my very best foot forward in what is my initial public offering.

I'd like to thank Hashem for providing for my family so amply on the Upper West Side of Manhattan over the last nine years. We arrived from Yerushalayim to a newly created position in an institution with a glorious past but a very uncertain future. I recall being warned that "I'd be lucky to survive six months," and somehow, almost miraculously, we have completed nine years serving the community.

I'd also like to thank *Mishpacha* magazine, managing editor Mrs. Shoshana Friedman and my good friend Sruli Besser for helping me grow as a writer. The forum the magazine has provided me with in the last few years in their GuestLines column has helped me realize how much I enjoy writing and that my words can have a profound impact and reach.

I'd like to thank my friends Michael and Allison Bromberg and Andrew and Shannon Penson, both of the Upper West Side, for being the great supporters of Torah that they are and helping me produce this Torah work.

I've had too many rabbinic influences to mention in this section (see my article in the book on this topic), but I'd like to acknowledge my *rebbi*, Rabbi Yaakov Friedman of Beitar, who guided me in my early years of marriage and under whom I had the privilege to study Torah. I still get tremendous *chizuk* upon receipt of the occasional letter of encouragement that arrives from Eretz Yisrael and on his visits to America or mine to Eretz Yisrael. It has now been a ten-plus-year relationship and I live my life following many of his guiding principles.

I'd also like to mention Rabbi Yehuda Kelemer, a prince of a man, who was my rabbi growing up and was such a quiet and unassuming role model. It was truly a privilege to grow up in his community, West Hempstead, New York.

I'd like to thank my siblings Jonathan and Yechiel for their friendship, love and support as well as my many siblings-in-law who are always inquiring as to my work and what I'm up to.

I'd like to acknowledge my maternal grandparents, Rabbi Meir and Tova Felman, *z"l*, who have been role models to me and inspired my career in the rabbinate, as well as my paternal grandparents, Mr. Abe and Fay Cohen, *z"l*.

I acknowledge my in-laws, Chief Rabbi Chaim and Annette Eisenberg of Vienna, Austria, who take great pride in my accomplishments and who so amply provided my wife with a wonderful home steeped in Torah knowledge and values.

I'd like to thank my wonderful parents, Mr. Milton and Shevi Cohen of West Hempstead, New York; Boynton Beach, Florida; and Jerusalem,

Israel, who are always there for me in any way I may need. They are my biggest fans and cheerleaders and there is nothing they wouldn't do for their children and grandchildren. My children are fortunate to have such special grandparents who live so close by (part of the year, anyway) and love to spend time with them.

I dedicate this first offering to my four children: Yedidya, Anaelle, Meir and Aharon. Each is the apple of my eye and what really makes life the great joy that it is. Anaelle in particular has kept this project a secret for a long time and will be most relieved that she can finally share it with her friends and her world. I'm sure she will also read it cover to cover, possibly in one sitting.

Finally, my dear wife and best friend, Ruchi. Ruchi is the compass that keeps me focused and ensures that I have the necessary environment to produce on behalf of the *klal*. Our amazing children are a tremendous tribute to her efforts and I'm most proud and inspired that she returned to school after four children to become a registered nurse. Ruchi is truly the one person on earth who almost completely understands the complexity and richness of contradictions that is me.

This book is ultimately a product or by-product of the wonderful life that we have built together and the many experiences and events that we have lived through and shared.

May we merit *yeshuos* and continued *nachas* from our beloved children until one hundred and twenty, together and in good health.

Dovid M. Cohen
Rosh Chodesh Kislev 5776
New York, New York

# FOREWORD

ews often teach by telling stories and learn by listening to them. The best stories for teaching and learning are not parables—though there are many wonderful parables. Rather, they are true stories—stories of the lived experience of men and women. The book you hold in your hands is a collection of such stories. From them, you will derive wisdom, though I must warn you that you will shed a tear or two along the way. (Don't worry, however, for you will also be rewarded by a chuckle now and then.)

Rabbi Dovid Cohen teaches us by sharing the stories of his life. He does more, however, than merely recount the facts. He interprets them and shares with us his reflections—invariably thoughtful and instructive—on their meaning. In doing so, he gives us a window into his life and, indeed, into his soul. But his stories are not just about him. They are about a people—his people, the Jewish people—a people whose rich traditions and deep spirituality, whose ancient books and modern sages, have shaped him from top to bottom. They give us a window into Jewishness.

Are these stories just for Jews, then?

No. Any gentile—at least any gentile who, like me, is willing to look up unfamiliar Yiddish or Hebrew words—has much to learn from R' Dovid's stories. And that is because the Jewish people, though "a people set apart," are a people with a mission in the world—a Divine mission. They are a people who are called to be "a light unto the nations." And, true to that mission, R' Dovid offers enlightenment—wisdom—to anyone who reads his stories thoughtfully and with a desire to learn.

Gentiles and Jews alike face the ordinary and sometimes extraordinary challenges that are the essence of leading a human life. We come into the world as children, full of wonder and needful of years of attentive care and nurturance. We are rational creatures, yet we have feelings and emotions. We experience joy and anger, happiness and hurt, affection and pain. We are required to earn our daily bread. We fall in love, marry and have children of our own. As we watch with joy our sons and daughters grow into fine men and women, we watch with sadness our beloved parents grow frail with age. We have in-laws. And neighbors. And friends. And people with whom we are not so friendly. We are, in a sense, locked into our own subjectivity, yet we can share our thoughts and feelings with others. We are individuals, yet members of communities. We are material beings, yet also spiritual beings to whom the Almighty has given a share of the Divine powers of reason and freedom of will. As the Bible says, "We are made in the image and likeness of G-d." Yet unlike G-d, we are mortal—mere "dust of the earth." And we live our lives in contemplation of our deaths.

These are, as I say, challenges common to all people in all times and at all places. Many traditions offer insights into them. But there is a special perspective—offering a unique body of wisdom—rooted in the experience of the Jews as G-d's chosen people.

The great pagan philosopher Plato taught that the "unexamined life is not worth living." R' Dovid teaches through his stories that it is worth living an examined life. He has encountered life's challenges—everything from changing professions to bringing up a disabled child—reflectively, looking for meaning, and finding it. How is it that he finds it, when so many others say they look for meaning yet find only meaninglessness? It is because R' Dovid does not stumble around in the dark. He has a light. It is the light of faith. It is in the light of faith that what is invisible in the darkness becomes clear.

Yet the rabbi's faith is not an uncritical faith. Nor does it make all the answers to life's challenges obvious or easy. It doesn't solve the great and sometimes painful mysteries, such as why the beautiful and brilliant daughter of a neighbor suddenly dies at the age of eighteen. But faith sustains him—and, he teaches, faith can sustain us—in hope and in the redeeming power of the G-d for whom we, as spiritual creatures, long. As we come to terms with life's challenges, seeking meaning in the light of faith, we find ourselves, in a sense, cooperating with G-d—praying, studying, following His commandments in caring not only for ourselves but for others. And in this cooperation, we experience not slavery, but rather freedom, the freedom that faith-sustaining hope alone can make possible.

Robert P. George
*McCormick Professor of Jurisprudence*
*and Director of the James Madison Program*
*in American Ideals and Institutions*
*Princeton University*

# INTRODUCTION

**A walk in the park:** *something that is very easy to do,
and usually pleasant (Cambridge Dictionary)*

**Ha-chaim zeh lo piknik:** *life isn't just a walk in the park
(loose translation)*

I heard the Hebrew expression above from a mentor of mine over twenty years ago and the words still very much resonate with me. For most of us, life isn't so easy. Even for those who appear to have it all, there are many behind-the-scenes pitfalls or potential obstacles lurking down the road. The challenge is one of patience and faith. Patience when things don't happen according to our schedule and faith that G-d not only has a plan for us, but also has the timing of that plan worked out down to the very millisecond.

Letting go of our dreams and ambitions and submitting to a higher authority is one of the most difficult things for the human ego. To admit that we're not in control is not easy to do. It makes us feel vulnerable and that is a place that many don't want to visit. I speak from experience about these issues. I married in my early thirties and then my first child was born with special needs. Professionally, I had big dreams and large ambitions that had not always succeeded. I waited, not so patiently, sharing a pulpit until my predecessor was finally ready to relinquish his pulpit of sixty years. I was also unsuccessful in my two attempts to move up to bigger more prominent positions. That being said, I try my best to keep my head down and just keep on moving forward.

Life isn't always fair and it certainly isn't a picnic. I look around and realize my challenges and frustrations are everywhere in different forms, and maybe for others a whole lot more painful and difficult. I wouldn't trade mine for someone else's.

My wife trained to be a professional doula or labor coach. In that process she came across the following mantra: "Hold the vision, trust the process." In the birthing context, it means the yearning for a natural birth story shouldn't be lost sight of, certainly not in the difficult moments when one is tempted by the epidural. One must cling to that vision while trusting a process that involves pain and disappointment. The pain is a signal that the body is opening and doing what it needs to. This unpleasant process will ultimately lead to that much anticipated birth.

When we occasionally travel by car with our four children, they always ask me, "How much longer?" or "Are we there yet?" I snicker to myself when they inquire, as they don't even have a firm grasp of time, and my answer wouldn't be meaningful to them as a barometer. They are really just expressing impatience or maybe even discomfort. Children live in the moment and they want things on their schedule. When that isn't provided, they tend to let you know they are dissatisfied.

No matter our age, we are all like children. In many realms, we ask ourselves or even others, *Why aren't we there yet?* Especially when logic dictates that we should have already arrived. At times, we continue to wait and sometimes we realize that we will never arrive in the way we had hoped. At those times, we need to gird for battle and ensure we aren't crushed for good. There will be other fields of play and other meaningful opportunities if we can allow ourselves to wipe the dust off and get off the mat.

This book explores areas of interest relating to Jewish life in particular and living in general. It gleans lessons from my own personal challenges as well as observations I have made about how others have handled their own. Some of the essays are just plain lessons from living an interesting, multifaceted life. I hope you enjoy, learn and hopefully grow from this journey. Most importantly though, understand that we are all still "in process," unfinished products if you will. I know this because we are all still here, which means G-d still has work for us to do and places for us to go. Maybe, just maybe, the reader will also question why exactly we are in such a hurry and maybe begin to enjoy the ride or the process just a little bit more. Finally, please remember that we are all much closer than we think or feel in any given moment of time; in fact, we're almost there!

# SECTION ONE

## The Rabbinate: Challenges and Opportunities in Serving Others

# MY REBBI'S REBBI

arrived at Yeshiva University as a sophomore and just watched him from a distance. The elderly, distinguished-looking man, with a full beard and traditional garb, was frail and always had someone accompanying him while he walked, ever so slowly. I yearned to approach and introduce myself, but, regrettably, fear held me back.

Rosh Yeshiva of RIETS,
Suvalker Rav and President
Ezras Torah, Rav Dovid Lifshitz

This great man was Rabbi Dovid Lifshitz, the Suvalker Rav, president of Ezras Torah and Rosh Yeshiva at Rabbi Isaac Elchanan Theological Seminary (RIETS) for nearly fifty years.

If we never spoke a word, why was I so intrigued by R' Dovid?

## CAMP RALEIGH: LIVINGSTON MANOR, NEW YORK

The answer can be understood by my first meaningful *rebbi/talmid* relationship.[1] I spent my summer after graduating high school as a counselor for

---

1    Rabbi Yitzchak Hutner, famed Rosh Yeshiva of Chaim Berlin, was hesitant to call any of

seventh grade boys. These boys had a *rebbi* that profoundly impacted their lives and came to visit them in camp. My campers discovered that their beloved *rebbi* and beloved counselor would be learning in the same Israeli institution the following year and decided to orchestrate a *shidduch,* or *chavrusa shaf.*

When I arrived in Israel, I was assigned an older *chavrusa* named Rabbi Ari Waxman. Every night for two hours I would learn *Maseches Sanhedrin* with R' Ari in his home while enjoying his wife's baked delicacies. There is little doubt I was the envy of most of my classmates that year for having such a desirable night *seder*—"*b'geshem u'beruach.*"

## MY FIRST REAL CHAVRUSA

Rabbi Waxman became my first *rebbi.* We spoke about many concepts in *hashkafah,* including *shidduchim,* living in Eretz Yisrael, career, serving in the army, the yeshiva world versus the *dati leumi* world and many other fascinating topics. I literally became a *ben bayis* and the first of what would soon be multitudes of other American boys arriving from Modern Orthodox homes who benefited immensely from his tutelage.

At some point, I noticed an arresting picture on his wall and discovered that his maternal grandfather was Rabbi Dovid Lifshitz. I didn't know at the time the magnitude or significance of the man on the wall, but eventually I began to realize how important R' Dovid was in R' Ari's life. When R' Ari attended RIETS, he actually lived with his grandparents in their apartment. He attended his grandfather's *shiur* and was his constant companion.

Toward the end of my second year in yeshiva in Israel, Rabbi Waxman and his wife were blessed with triplets—their first children. Two of them

his students *talmidim.* In fact, he would say that Rabbi Akiva Eiger also didn't call students *talmidim.* Rabbi Hutner used effusive language in his printed letters calling his students beloved, like a child, but he never used the term *talmid.*

were boys and R' Ari had to prepare a *shtikel Torah* for the *brisim*. Together, we studied and prepared Torah related to *milah* and *priah* from the published *shiurim* of his grandfather. It was the culmination of our learning relationship and I felt welcomed into his intimate relationship with his revered *zaide*.

Rabbi Dovid Lifshitz died on the 9th of Tammuz in 1993, but R' Dovid would continue to play a major role in my life for many years to come.

## FAIR LAWN, NEW JERSEY

In 1995, I was assigned a rabbinic internship that catapulted me toward the rabbinate. My assigned mentor was Rabbi Benjamin Yudin of Fair Lawn, New Jersey. I followed Rabbi Yudin everywhere and learned from one of the masters how to become an effective and influential pulpit rabbi. I saw some incredible things. Those who know Rabbi Yudin will understand that being with him was truly the experience of a lifetime.

Rabbi Yudin imparted to me the importance of having a *rebbi* and imbibing Torah from every corner. He would regularly converse in learning with Rabbi Elya Chaim Swerdloff of Paterson, New Jersey, Rabbi Aharon Kreiser, of Lakewood, New Jersey, as well as with Rabbi Hershel Schachter and Rabbi Mordechai Willig of RIETS. Interestingly, his prime *rebbi* in his formative yeshiva years was none other than ... Rabbi Dovid Lifshitz.

## BRIS MILAH SHIMUSH

One anecdote about R' Dovid that I heard from Rabbi Yudin really stands out in my mind. The story took place at the *bris* of one of the Yudin boys. R' Dovid was present, of course. After the *milah*, R' Dovid made his way directly to Rebbetzin Yudin to assure her that everything had gone smoothly and the baby was fine. Rabbi Yudin endeavored to bring this type of *chesed* and sensitivity to his own *rabbanus*, and it is something I try to do as well in my *kehillah*.

## NEO-CHASSIDUS

In 2000, I began what would be a four-year stint practicing corporate law. For the first time in over a decade I was completely beyond the walls of the *beis midrash*. I needed badly to be connected to something that would strengthen me and keep me spiritually sound. Toward the end of my time in Fair Lawn, Rabbi Moshe Weinberger of Aish Kodesh in Woodmere, New York, was a guest lecturer in the shul. I had the opportunity to drive him from Woodmere to Fair Lawn and back, and (thanks to massive traffic tie-ups!) I was able to spend about three hours with him in private conversation. We connected in a profound way; I still give *divrei Torah* I gleaned from that conversation. He also spoke to me about his *rebbi*—who, it turned out, was ... Rabbi Dovid Lifshitz.

> I NEEDED BADLY TO BE CONNECTED TO SOMETHING THAT WOULD STRENGTHEN ME AND KEEP ME SPIRITUALLY SOUND.

> *I recall Rabbi Weinberger speaking of R' Dovid longingly, with a palpable yearning. He told me about the time he was driving R' Dovid somewhere and shared a vort with him. R' Dovid was so enthused by what he heard that he required Rabbi Weinberger to stop the car and repeat it to him while they sat on the side of the road. After hearing the vort again, R' Dovid began singing, in a niggun of sorts, "Moshe emes v'Toraso emes." The story was a striking example of R' Dovid's enthusiasm for his lifeblood—"the heilege Torah."*

Thankfully, Rabbi Weinberger began to take an interest in me and in my development, and I was invited to join a late Thursday night *chaburah* in Maharal with him for a number of years while I practiced law. This kept me afloat as I worked endless hours in challenging environments. Rabbi Weinberger played a significant role in guiding me through various life challenges during that time.

When I met my wife, I decided to leave the law and spend my initial years of marriage in full-time learning. I was accepted by a challenging *kollel* and was a bit nervous, as I'd be one of the oldest people in the institution. I spoke with Rabbi Weinberger and his advice to me was, "Don't be embarrassed to ask someone

> "DON'T BE EMBARRASSED TO ASK SOMEONE YOUNGER THAN YOU TO EXPLAIN THE *TOSAFOS* AGAIN IF YOU DON'T UNDERSTAND IT THE FIRST TIME."

younger than you to explain the *Tosafos* again if you don't understand it the first time." This was a clear *mesorah* of *ahavas haTorah* from his *rebbi*.

## THE WORLD OF CHAIM BERLIN AND RABBI HUTNER

In 2006, I became rabbi of the Young Israel of the West Side in Manhattan and was tasked with taking over the reins of a historic and illustrious *kehillah* from the revered and renowned Rabbi Emanuel Gettinger. I had an opportunity to speak with Rabbi Ari Waxman during the initial stages of assuming the role and he was interested in knowing about Rabbi Gettinger. He explained that Rabbi Gettinger had replaced his grandfather R' Dovid as president of Ezras Torah after R' Dovid's *petirah* and that they had worked closely together for many years. In fact, I heard stated at Rabbi Gettinger's *levayah* that for many years, R' Dovid didn't make a move regarding Ezras Torah without the insight and support of Rabbi Gettinger. This was despite his being much older than Rabbi Gettinger. Amazingly, the R' Dovid connection hadn't left me.

More than twenty years have passed since the *petirah* of R' Dovid, and I see how resoundingly accurate are the words of Chazal: the righteous, even after death, are very much alive and present.[2] Through my connection with four very different personalities, I've merited to capture a tiny bit of the essence of one of the greats of the previous generation.

> THROUGH MY CONNECTION WITH FOUR VERY DIFFERENT PERSONALITIES, I'VE MERITED TO CAPTURE A TINY BIT OF THE ESSENCE OF ONE OF THE GREATS OF THE PREVIOUS GENERATION.

Maybe—just possibly—I carry the name Dovid as a hint of what was to be the profound influence on my life—my "grand *rebbi*," Rabbi Dovid Lifshitz, *yehi zichro baruch*.[3]

---

2     *Berachos* 18a.
3     Interestingly, my given name at my *bris* was Yisroel Moshe after my paternal great-grandfather. My English given name was David. My maternal grandfather, Rabbi Meir Felman, thought it would be odd to have non-matching English and Hebrew names and therefore encouraged my parents to add the name Dovid about a month after my *bris*. Rabbi Yaakov Meir Shechter of Breslov removed the Yisroel from my name about thirty years later, leaving me with the current Hebrew name, Dovid Moshe. Changing a name is a very serious thing and only should be done in consultation with very great rabbinic guidance. It's fascinating to me that my name has been changed twice.

# THE NOBLEST
# PROFESSION
# OF THEM ALL

My father-in-law, Chief Rabbi Chaim Eisenberg of Vienna, Austria, who has spent his entire career in the rabbinate, is fond of saying, "If everybody likes you, then you aren't a rabbi, but if no one likes you, you aren't a *mentch*!"

"IF EVERYBODY LIKES YOU,
THEN YOU AREN'T A RABBI,
BUT IF NO ONE LIKES YOU,
YOU AREN'T A *MENTCH*!"

## WHY NOT BE A DOCTOR?

You'd be hard-pressed to find the proverbial Jewish mother yearning for her son to become a pulpit rabbi. After all, it's not the most financially lucrative field and the hours can be pretty grueling—not to mention the politics. My mother supported my passion for the rabbinate with the condition that I have a "back-up" degree, just "in case." As the daughter of a rabbi, she knows of what she speaks.[4]

YOU'D BE HARD-PRESSED TO FIND THE PROVERBIAL JEWISH MOTHER YEARNING FOR HER SON TO BECOME A PULPIT RABBI.

Still, although not easy, I've come to appreciate the unique privilege that I've had for over fifteen years now; the honor of communal service and the myriad opportunities to be a *mentch*, or as translated into English, a person with concern for others.

## HOW MANY ATTEND YOUR CLASSES?

Years ago, in a rabbinic training course, I heard a prominent pulpit rabbi comment that "the only thing worse than having nobody attend your *shiur* is having one person attend." A few years back, I actually observed a rabbi refuse to give a *shiur*, because only seven people had shown up. I guess we all have different ego thresholds.

THE ONLY THING WORSE THAN HAVING NOBODY ATTEND YOUR *SHIUR* IS HAVING ONE PERSON ATTEND.

However, I'd beg to differ with both of these *rabbanim*.

The role of a rabbi is to build personal relationships with as many of his congregants as possible. Being a *mentch* dictates showing respect to any individual making the effort to come hear what the *rav* may have to say on any given evening. It's not about quantity of relationships, but quality of relationships and a rapport being developed. Even the great Moshe Rabbeinu had the most humble of origins, tending to individual sheep, before being selected to be the *manhig* of Klal Yisrael.[5]

---

4    I once heard the son of a rabbi thank his father's *kehillah* for treating his father so respectfully that he too desired to pursue the rabbinate, which he in fact did. Sadly, this is an anomalous case as many children of rabbis become all too aware of the less idealistic parts of the profession and often steer clear of the field.

5    Granted, this isn't for everybody and sometimes we find very scholarly *rabbanim* who lack the necessary people skills to connect with the community.

## WHO AM I?

I once heard a beautiful kabbalistic interpretation of the word "*Ani*."[6] The Hebrew word for "I" is comprised of three distinct letters. The *aleph* stands for the individual, the *yud* at the end of the word stands for the community (with the numerical value of ten representing the power of *tzibbur*), and the *nun* in the middle stands for the fifty rungs of *binah* (wisdom) that manifest in the realms of Torah.

The task of a *ben Torah* (and a rabbi in particular) is to use his intellectual and emotional acumen, his infusion of *binah* (wisdom), to include within his "I" the broader community. It takes much perception and insight to figure out how to effectively let each congregant or member feel as though they are part of your nuclear family. Often, the bigger the person in terms of spiritual prowess and accomplishment, the more all-encompassing and inclusive their "I" tends to be. *Gedolei Yisrael* feel the pain and anguish as well as the joy of the multitudes that seek out their guidance and sage advice. They daven for the entirety of Klal Yisrael. The model rabbi demonstrates to his entire *kehillah* that he feels they are part of his own family.[7]

> GEDOLEI YISRAEL FEEL THE PAIN AND ANGUISH AS WELL AS THE JOY OF THE MULTITUDES THAT SEEK OUT THEIR GUIDANCE AND SAGE ADVICE. THEY DAVEN FOR THE ENTIRETY OF KLAL YISRAEL.

## THE EFFECTIVE RABBI

A colleague shared the following insight with me.[8] He homiletically explained the verse in the first *brachah* of every *Shemoneh Esrei*, "*Gomel chasadim tovim v'koneh ha-kol*—G-d Who bestows beneficial

---

6    Rabbi Zev Leff said this in a *teshuvah drashah* that I heard him give in Yeshivat Sha'alvim in 1990.

7    When I trained under Rabbi Yudin in Fair Lawn, New Jersey, he insisted on learning with each bar mitzvah boy and helping each one prepare a *drashah*. When I implored him to allow me to relieve some of the burden, he answered that this is how he incorporates each young man into his family and it isn't something that he plans to share or give up on.

8    Rabbi Shaul Robinson, rabbi of Lincoln Square Synagogue in Manhattan, told this over to me in the name of former Chief Rabbi Jonathan Sacks of Great Britain.

kindness and creates everything," as a directive to the rabbi. If the rabbi is expressing loving kindness to his flock, then he can acquire them as his own or acquire "everything." If the spiritual leader is erudite, a great speaker and a deft politician, but people don't feel him being "*gomel chassadim tovim*," then he will not have acquired them as his followers.

I often find it awkward when the *kehillah* waits for me to finish my *Shemoneh Esrei*. I try not to place a burden on the community, particularly during the week, when people need to get to work. It is true—rabbis often daven slower than others in the *minyan*, but our davening is weighed down by an additional factor: rabbis are privy to confidential information. We know about the various couples undergoing treatments for infertility, people undergoing chemotherapy, people out of work, and people desperately in need of a *shidduch*. It's a heavy burden that we carry and some of my private davening time each day is devoted to my flock that is in need. Of course, I call them and follow their progress, but it's the quiet tears and intense yearning on their behalf that solidifies our bond and incorporates them as part of me. The irony is that they are holding me up—and not vice versa as is sometimes perceived.

> THE IRONY IS THAT THEY ARE HOLDING ME UP–AND NOT VICE VERSA, AS IS SOMETIMES PERCEIVED.

## HAVE YOU HAD YOUR YEARLY SPIRITUAL?

One Pesach season a few years ago, congregants came to my office to appoint me as their agent to sell their *chametz*. Many people shared difficulties that they were experiencing and a few even broke down in tears. When I discussed this with a friend, he commented that it solidifies his feeling that just as many of us go for a yearly medical "physical," each of us should also visit his rabbi for a yearly "spiritual." I subsequently shared this conversation in a Shabbos morning *drashah*.

> JUST AS MANY OF US GO FOR A YEARLY MEDICAL "PHYSICAL," EACH OF US SHOULD ALSO VISIT HIS RABBI FOR A YEARLY "SPIRITUAL."

A few weeks later, I was confronted with a rabbinic conundrum. A member, who was soon leaving the *kehillah* to move elsewhere, had lost his father. I was away in Los Angeles and had missed the funeral and would be left with just a Friday to pay a shivah visit. The problem was that my congregant was sitting shivah in Philadelphia. Despite the urge to skip the shivah call (and despite my rationalizations that he would soon be moving away anyway), I decided that a "*mentch*" makes this shivah call in person.[9] So I invested significant time and resources to travel back and forth before Shabbos.

I was in for a real shocker at the shivah house. My congregant wasn't the most devout listener to my weekly speeches and I was caught off guard when he referenced a recent one. He commented that he felt my remark a few weeks back about people "breaking down" during the *chametz* transaction was a reference to him, which was in fact partially true. He then poignantly said, "But Rabbi, you got it wrong. The 'spiritual' that you spoke of must take place every six months as opposed to once a year."

I was surprised that he had listened, and even more so, inspired by his retort. When we are authentic and genuine and show we truly care, we often touch people without even realizing it.

## THE REBBETZIN

Ultimately, no rabbi can be successful in his mission without a wonderful *rebbetzin*. These women come in many different styles. Some are "typical" or more naturally cut out for such a role and others less so. No matter the public persona, you can rest assured that

---

9    I had another situation where a congregant was sitting in Connecticut and the weather was poor. To her credit, my wife pushed me to go in person and not just make a phone call. I was rewarded by meeting the congregant's one-hundred-year-old mother who showered me with blessings for my efforts.

there is a wonderful partner cheering on and encouraging the rabbi to make the extra phone call or go the extra mile. I recently missed a wedding due to an illness and had called the *chassan* to profusely apologize beforehand. It was my wife who asked me the day after the wedding if I had called the *chassan* again. I asked her why. She responded, "To show that you care and that you're thinking about him and to see if he needs anything." I married well.

These women are the anchors that keep everything running at home and make the quiet sacrifices that enable their husbands to be engaged in the lives of others.

## SHALOM BAYIS–NARROW AND BROAD

There is a classic anecdote of a couple that agreed before marriage that the man would handle the *"ruchniyus"* and the woman the *"gashmiyus."* This way, they theoretically would never fight over anything. Ironically, what they were left to argue over was what issues fall into which category.

*Rabbanim* presumably should leave the physical to the congregants and engage in the spiritual. However, truly passionate dedicated leaders understand that every aspect of a *"kodesh"* operation, no matter how mundane, is really subsumed under the heading of a spiritual concern. The great leaders of our people understood that just as every detail is of spiritual import, so is every *neshamah* of critical import. So in truth, my dear mother encouraged me to finish my law degree and I did practice four years of corporate law to boot. Though ultimately, nothing beats what I'm doing now—being a *mentch* for a living!

> THE GREAT LEADERS OF OUR PEOPLE UNDERSTOOD THAT JUST AS EVERY DETAIL IS OF SPIRITUAL IMPORT, SO IS EVERY *NESHAMAH* OF CRITICAL IMPORT.

# INDELIBLE MEMORIES

t is, for me, a "tale of two cities," two life stories, set years apart. Sudden unexpected tragedy has a way of just taking the wind out of your sails. We wake up in the morning expecting a regular day, but the reality becomes the ultimate nightmare. In truth, I was but an observer in both situations—and yet carry some of the trauma of both with me to this day.

## RABBINIC TRAINING AND THEN SOME

Many years ago, I was invited to serve as intern and then assistant rabbi to Rabbi Binyomin Yudin in Fair Lawn, New Jersey. About six months into my tenure, there was a tragedy that profoundly impacted the community. Various members of the congregation were commuting to work and their train crashed on the way. Two members sat near each other, one of whom was severely injured while the other was killed instantaneously upon impact.

David Stern was a prominent attorney and activist. He had a wife and five daughters. He had made a significant positive impact on the community. The news trickled in on a Friday and I found myself in the thick of

things over the course of the weekend as the news was digested and
funeral arrangements were made.
It was difficult meeting his family
(for the first time) in the context
of enormous grief, and I even felt

IT WAS DIFFICULT MEETING HIS
FAMILY (FOR THE FIRST TIME) IN THE
CONTEXT OF ENORMOUS GRIEF, AND
I EVEN FELT A TAD GUILTY FOR THEIR
TRAGEDY SERVING AS MY RABBINIC
"TRAINING GROUNDS."

a tad guilty for their tragedy serving as my rabbinic "training grounds." I
felt a bit better when I found myself helping to comfort the three younger
daughters, away from the traffic in the home.

## SUDDEN UNEXPECTED CHOICES

There are many decisions that need to be made after a tragic loss. Most
often, those directly impacted are not best equipped to contemplate those
choices, and yet these decisions need to be made—often very quickly. There
is a Divine hand that ultimately helps navigate those interim moments and
somehow gets the family through
by surrounding them with the appropriate people. In this specific
scenario, there was the added complexity of convincing authorities
not to perform an autopsy—efforts
that proved successful.

THERE IS A DIVINE HAND THAT
ULTIMATELY HELPS NAVIGATE THOSE
INTERIM MOMENTS AND SOMEHOW
GETS THE FAMILY THROUGH BY
SURROUNDING THEM WITH THE
APPROPRIATE PEOPLE.

After this tragedy, I became a *ben bayis* of sorts in that home. I would
often be invited for Shabbos meals, and I recall attending the weddings
of two of the daughters. Life does go on and the widow remarried and the
three young girls I met at the shivah house are now mothers themselves.
Yet every now and then, my mind travels back to Fair Lawn, New Jersey,
and I see myself as a twenty-two-year-old young rabbi-in-training, attempting to grapple with the unfathomable.

## BOUNCING BACK SLOWLY

People tend to regroup and move on from such painful episodes, but reflecting on those initial moments of loss, it amazes me that it is indeed possible to recover. The gentleman who survived the train crash underwent a very long recuperative period. He had another child after the accident and named him after David Stern.

I've lost contact with all the "primary players" at this point, but I do carry them with me. The raw emotions of that time in my life are indelibly etched upon my heart.

Much has transpired in my life since my five-year training stint in Fair Lawn, New Jersey. Most significantly, I am married, have my own family and have a pulpit of my own. Although I am now a very different person, it amazes me how this event remains for me frozen in time. It is as if a piece of me will always be at that place, in that time—potentially even years from now. It is overwhelming to contemplate how transformative a moment in time can actually be, even when just an observer.

> ALTHOUGH I AM NOW A VERY DIFFERENT PERSON, IT AMAZES ME HOW THIS EVENT REMAINS FOR ME FROZEN IN TIME.

I experienced my own "sudden loss" upon the birth of my first child, Yedidya Shlomo. I don't mean to compare it to a death, *chas v'shalom*, because that is the furthest thing from the truth; our special-needs child has brought us much life and joy.

## FANTASY TO REALITY

What we did lose was the child we were hoping for: the idyllic child who would learn in high-level *yeshivos* and make us extremely proud—the one who would marry and produce future generations of *talmidei chachamim*, *anshei emes* and *zera kodesh* in Klal Yisrael.

On some level, sudden loss is about shattered expectations and feeling intense vulnerability—realizing that life will now move in a different direction from what we expected or anticipated, and that no matter what we may fool ourselves into thinking, we really have almost no control over life events.

> ON SOME LEVEL, SUDDEN LOSS IS ABOUT SHATTERED EXPECTATIONS AND FEELING INTENSE VULNERABILITY.

Sudden shifts in life are plain hard. Sometimes we see people who have suffered a loss far less challenging than death struggling with it with as much confusion as those who have suffered extreme grief. Disappointment, especially of a sudden nature, is of the greatest challenges to adapt to.

## FALSE SENSE OF ENTITLEMENT

Unexpected loss jars us from the expectation that we are entitled to another day of life, a perfect child—or any child for that matter—or that fairy tale ending. As we recover, we re-orient and begin to appreciate how every moment along the trajectory of an expected life span is really an important part of our life journey. After all, no aspect of tomorrow is guaranteed and yesterday isn't proof of a tomorrow.[10]

> AFTER ALL, NO ASPECT OF TOMORROW IS GUARANTEED AND YESTERDAY ISN'T PROOF OF A TOMORROW.

## AGAIN? NOT AGAIN!

On Chanukah, I had a déjà vu experience. My neighbor was supposed to sponsor *shalosh seudos* in our shul. He isn't the type of person to disappear on an event he sponsored, so we were a bit concerned when he didn't show up. After Shabbos, as I was getting ready to head out to a yearly family Chanukah party, I went upstairs to find out if he was feeling okay. I was instructed by his son to call the hospital. After I called, I immediately headed over to a nearby hospital—not yet fully sure what had transpired.

Upon arrival, I discovered the absolute worst possible scenario. Shoshana Macey, our neighbor's one-of-a-kind eighteen-year-old daughter had suddenly and unexpectedly passed away on Shabbos afternoon. Just three days earlier, Shoshana had asked me to help her with a Torah paper she was

> IN THE BLINK OF AN EYE, SHE WAS GONE–TAKEN FROM US WITH NO WARNING AND NO EXPLANATION.

---

10    *Shabbos* 153a discusses doing *teshuvah* one day before you die, which translates into daily as nobody knows when they will meet their ultimate demise.

writing about marriage for a course at Touro College. A few weeks before that, she babysat our kids on a moment's notice. In the blink of an eye, she was gone—taken from us with no warning and no explanation.

## ALL GROWN UP WITH MUCH RESPONSIBILITY

This time, I was a seasoned rabbi, and it was my sole responsibility. You can never be fully prepared for something like this, but the experience years ago alerted me to the potential issues and intricacies. I knew that there was nothing that I could possibly say that would bring comfort. I may have experienced a sudden loss of sorts and closely observed others in such situations, but every human is built differently and no experience is exactly comparable to another. This is why I cringe when I'm sitting in a shivah home and hear those most irritating words: "I know exactly what you are going through." Actually, no—you don't. Every experience is unique. Whenever I delude myself into thinking that my experiences help me understand a bit of another's pain, I quickly remind myself that I can't truly touch the inner-workings of another human being. I can be moved and impacted, but can't totally absorb another's reality.

> I KNEW THAT THERE WAS NOTHING THAT I COULD POSSIBLY SAY THAT WOULD BRING COMFORT.

> THIS IS WHY I CRINGE WHEN I'M SITTING IN A SHIVAH HOME AND HEAR THOSE MOST IRRITATING WORDS: "I KNOW EXACTLY WHAT YOU ARE GOING THROUGH." ACTUALLY, NO–YOU DON'T.

Once again, I became very close with the grieving family, a bond intensified by what we shared and went through together. Shoshana's younger twin brothers love to play with my boys and have been incredibly helpful to our family.

## SILENCE WITH SOME ACHE

You never ever speak of the things you see and hear in those initial moments and days. You file them deep inside and seal them up. You carry them with you and they change you forever, and strangely, they can reappear from the deep recesses of your memory on very short notice. Life is just a drop less joyous, as you are keenly aware of the intense suffering of another human being, people that you have grown to care deeply about.

This most recent experience again feels like it will linger for many years. It is something that I anticipate carrying with me. I wish I had the tools to magically make the pain of others go away or to somehow change the story. I hope with the passage of time the pain and ache will dull for those most deeply affected and connected.

We all yearn for the day when Hashem will wipe away all the tears[11] and we can get a glimpse of what He was thinking with these sudden tragedies. Until that day, I will carry the memories of those terrible and life-altering moments deep within me.

> I WISH I HAD THE TOOLS TO MAGICALLY MAKE THE PAIN OF OTHERS GO AWAY OR TO SOMEHOW CHANGE THE STORY.

---

11    *Yeshayahu* 25:8.

# MISSING RABBI GETTINGER

The Talmudic term used to describe sunset is *"shkiah."*[12] There is much controversy surrounding the definition of this period of time and much ink has been spilled explaining the various debates, nuances and opinions. One of the works surrounding this topic, the *Menach Yoma*,[13] was authored by Rabbi Emmanuel Gettinger, who was my predecessor as rabbi of the Young Israel of the West Side. Rabbi Gettinger wrote this manuscript about thirty-five years ago when he took a sabbatical from the shul. He merited publishing it only much more recently.

## SHKIAH?!

I still remember vividly the initial time I casually and innocently

---

12    *Berachos* 2b.

13    The name of the *sefer* comes from *Targum Onkeles Bereishis* (3:8) describing the direction from which Hashem calls to Adam and Chava after the sin of the *Eitz haDaas*, the Tree of Knowledge.

mentioned the term "*shkiah*" in his presence. He quizzically looked at me and said loudly, "*Shkiah*! What is *shkiah*?" I can still hear his voice ringing in my ear today. It was a trick question and an opening to discuss his favorite topic. This exchange happened numerous times over our years together.

Rabbi Gettinger teaching Torah at the ceremony in honor of the publishing of his magnum opus "Menach Yoma" on March 6, 2011 at the home of Sinclair and Sharon Haberman on the Upper West Side.

I met the revered (and famed) Rabbi Gettinger towards the *shkiah* of his life. He had already reached the stage of "*gevuros*" (eighty years), as he liked to refer to it. A man who completed *Shas* at the tender age of seventeen—one can only imagine how much I missed in only meeting him when he was in his early eighties. In truth, I walked away from our first meeting thinking he was going on fifty. The man was sharp as ever, spry and incredibly alert. I wished him well, but honestly was discouraged—as I never thought I'd have the chance at Young Israel to lead my own shul.

> A MAN WHO COMPLETED *SHAS* AT THE TENDER AGE OF SEVENTEEN—ONE CAN ONLY IMAGINE HOW MUCH I MISSED IN ONLY MEETING HIM WHEN HE WAS IN HIS EARLY EIGHTIES.

## TWILIGHT ZONE

Rabbi Joseph B. Soloveitchik commented that *bein hashmashos*, the twilight period between sunset and nightfall, is a combination period comprised of aspects of both day and night.[14] Conceptually, he argued it was defined as a new entity, distinct from both periods, something entirely new: not really day or night. It embodies a new unfamiliar reality that raises various intricacies in Jewish law.

Sadly, at the Young Israel of the West Side, the months leading up to Purim 5775 were *bein hashmashos*. Rabbi Gettinger was very much still with us, but in reality not with us at all. It wasn't the daytime, as when he led Young Israel for sixty years, but thankfully not the absolute darkness of nighttime either, as he slowly recovered in Chicago from a serious stroke. It amazes me how the essence of a person can be so imbedded within the walls of an institution. He was nowhere to be found—and at the same time everywhere. To this day, when certain people refer to the "Rabbi," I need to double-check and clarify if they mean him or me.

## TWO RABBIS / DOUBLE TROUBLE

My initial years at Young Israel as Rabbi Gettinger's associate rabbi were another *bein hashmashos* of sorts. We overlapped and shared rabbinical duties. At first, he spoke on Yom Kippur, gave the big *Shabbos Shuvah* and *Shabbos HaGadol drashos*, he was *makri* on Rosh Hashanah and he did *mechiras chametz* for the *kehillah*. He also remained the *posek* for the shul, and I often had to explain his unique halachic views to a young *kehillah* that didn't always understand his approach. It was a tricky period for me. I was in my mid-thirties and felt mature enough to handle my own *kehillah*—and yet I was still second-in-command to someone who was very much in command.

HE ALSO REMAINED THE *POSEK* FOR THE SHUL, AND I OFTEN HAD TO EXPLAIN HIS UNIQUE HALACHIC VIEWS TO A YOUNG *KEHILLAH* THAT DIDN'T ALWAYS UNDERSTAND HIS APPROACH.

---

14     *Shiurim L'zecher Abba Mori, z"l* 1:97–104.

Rabbi Gettinger, a prime and early disciple of Rabbi Yitzchak Hutner of Yeshivas Chaim Berlin, very much demanded *kavod haTorah*.[15] He was strict in its applications and demanded it of everybody, from great scholars to the simplest *baal ha-bayis*. He wasn't interested in hearing about "new" ways of doing things or what the recently arriving new generation wanted or expected out of the shul. He knew what was right and he didn't feel the need to explain himself. He also demanded that I, as a (young) rabbi, demand *kavod haTorah* as well. When I'd call his home and introduce myself as Dovid Cohen (to either him or his indomitable, illustrious *rebbetzin*), they would immediately respond with a very strong and subtle message of "Hello, Rabbi Cohen."

HE WASN'T INTERESTED IN HEARING ABOUT "NEW" WAYS OF DOING THINGS OR WHAT THE RECENTLY ARRIVING NEW GENERATION WANTED OR EXPECTED OUT OF THE SHUL.

It took only my second week at work to receive my first (of many!) firm rebuke from him. We used to learn *b'chavrusa* in my initial year and the sessions were fascinating. The stylistic clash between my yeshiva training and his more scholarly approach was something to behold. The sessions went on for hours, until frankly, the demands of my time precluded continuing. Early on in my tenure, he used a verse we were learning together to scold me and remind me about what topics are better left unaddressed in a public forum. I was a little scared of his ire or wrath and it didn't help that the young congregants enjoyed seeing me figuratively squirm next to a small figure of towering stature, waiting to see if I was up to the challenge.

I WAS A LITTLE SCARED OF HIS IRE OR WRATH AND IT DIDN'T HELP THAT THE YOUNG CONGREGANTS ENJOYED SEEING ME FIGURATIVELY SQUIRM NEXT TO A SMALL FIGURE OF TOWERING STATURE, WAITING TO SEE IF I WAS UP TO THE CHALLENGE.

---

15      Rabbeinu Bachya in *Kad Hakemach*, section on *yirah*, has a fascinating linkage between awe of G-d and awe of Torah scholars. He explains that reverence for the scholar in the deepest sense is really an expression of reverence for the Almighty.

## EARNING MY STRIPES

The first three years were difficult. At one point, I even tried to leave. I began every public address with "*Bi-reshus haRav*,"[16] and although respectful and appropriate, it made it difficult to escape his lofty shadow. Eventually, something shifted in a positive way. I don't know exactly when it happened, but I began to really gain his trust. He slowly began to relinquish his hold on things and there was a marked shift in his attitude toward me.

**EVENTUALLY, SOMETHING SHIFTED IN A POSITIVE WAY.**

As time went on, I really enjoyed just spending time with him, schmoozing, hearing about what Young Israel used to be. He would always ask about my family and my parents. He loved my kids and my kids really adored him. He would show my Meir Simcha his telescope and would listen to my Anaelle repeat the entire Purim story to him. When I'd ask Anaelle who her favorite rabbi was, she'd always first respond Rabbi Gettinger. Thankfully, her Abba was always a close second.

**WHEN I'D ASK ANAELLE WHO HER FAVORITE RABBI WAS, SHE'D ALWAYS FIRST RESPOND RABBI GETTINGER.**

Rabbi Cohen and Rabbi Gettinger walking together and talking about life on the corner of Broadway and 93rd street of the Upper West Side of Manhattan in February 2013. Abe Altman snapped the picture of us.

---

16    The same *Kad Hakemach* mentions that it is appropriate to ask permission before speaking in front of a Torah scholar.

## BROADENING MY OWN PERSPECTIVE

I began to change as well. Rather than see him as an obstacle or a hindrance to my success, I began to appreciate the privilege I had to learn from a giant of a man. I had a very unique perspective indeed. To be so close to a man who had touched the greatness of Rabbi Henkin, Rabbi Hutner and his father-in-law, Rabbi Riff. Rabbi Gettinger was from a different generation, and yet so much a part of ours. Amazingly, I had a very unique view and role that nobody else ever was privy to nor could totally understand.[17]

Rabbi Gettinger showing my Meir Simcha in 2011 how to angle his prized telescope. Photo in the Gettinger living room overlooking Riverside Drive on the Upper West Side.

## THE WRONG TITLE

Rabbi Gettinger wasn't a big shmoozer. In my mind—and maybe to others—he was a Rosh Yeshiva trapped as a pulpit rabbi.

He always enjoyed telling me the story of how Rabbi Moshe Feinstein,

---

17    In the history of the Young Israel of the West Side, there have been only three rabbis. Rabbi Gettinger formally served from 1954 until 2015. I joined him in 2006 and basically ran the shul soon after. Rabbi Yaakov Sprung served for one year (1970) when Rabbi Gettinger went on sabbatical to Israel. He is the tricky answer to the trivia question as to who the third rabbi in the history of YIWS was.

the *posek ha-dor*, was called "Rosh Yeshiva" and how Rabbi Joseph B. Soloveitchik, who was a classic Rosh Yeshiva, was called "The Rav."

They are different roles and different skill sets and sometimes the role or title isn't always apt in describing the person. It wasn't always the grandest fit for him, dealing with people way beneath his lofty halachic and learning standards. My recent recollections of the man are of warm embraces and, even (once!) a kiss on the cheek, but I know he wasn't always this tender, at least not in the shul. He was warm and welcoming if you pursued him, but it wasn't the modern day glad-handling rabbi at the *Kiddush* type of thing.[18]

## A NEXUS OF WORLDS

As I reflect, he was really a *bein hashmashos* incarnate. He fit into two worlds comfortably, Yeshivish and Modern Orthodox, and yet he didn't really fit into either. He attended Columbia University and had advanced degrees in mathematics and engineering and did *kiruv* way before any modern-day college campus organization or the institutionalization of *kiruv* as a movement. His devotion and reverence for his *rebbetzin* was spectacular and exemplary. In fact, the earliest and sternest piece of advice he gave me was to invest the money and make sure my *rebbetzin* had adequate help in her new role.

> HE FIT INTO TWO WORLDS COMFORTABLY, YESHIVISH AND MODERN ORTHODOX, AND YET HE DIDN'T REALLY FIT INTO EITHER.

He was very computer savvy and used technology very effectively for a man of his age, yet he was also the quintessential "*ish ha-tefillah.*" He could be quiet and still, and he could be engaged and vociferous. To watch him daven so slowly and carefully, reciting each and every word was something to behold. He also loved to recite *Sefer Tehillim*. He was an amalgamation of different time periods in our history and different currents of Orthodoxy.

> HE WAS AN AMALGAMATION OF DIFFERENT TIME PERIODS IN OUR HISTORY AND DIFFERENT CURRENTS OF ORTHODOXY.

---

18    An older congregant shared that the membership would prod him to walk around and greet people at the *Kiddush*, but he didn't feel it was dignified. If you approached him, he certainly would warmly greet you and engage you.

## WHEN DO YOU END SHABBOS?

It fascinates me how different institutions end Shabbos at different times on the Upper West Side of Manhattan. People are always in a hurry to get somewhere and often choose the "early times" for *Maariv*. As Rabbi Gettinger's magnum opus was elucidating the opinion of Rabbeinu Tam,[19] he was never in a rush to end Shabbos.[20] This devotion to Rabbeinu Tam's view, or at least his novel interpretation of it, beautifully describes how we at Young Israel feel now.

Our spiritual guide, the mentor of so many for so long, represented to us *kedushah*, being apart, but also being together with us providing illumination and light. We missed his indomitable presence and prayed that he wouldn't take leave of us. At the same time, it was hard not to realize that Shabbos was ebbing away, that he likely would not return to us. He left us the legacy of Rabbeinu Tam, and we davened and held out as long as possible, until the sun ultimately set and a new halachic reality or day began.

On Shushan Purim 5775, he quietly left this world and entered the world that is totally Shabbos. May his memory be for us as an everlasting blessing, as our Torah world and certainly the Young Israel of the West Side will never be the same.

---

19    According to Rabbi Yehuda in *Shabbos* 34b, *bein hashmashos* lasts thirteen-and-a-half minutes. In *Pesachim* 94a, however, the same Rabbi Yehuda maintains that *bein hashmashos* lasts seventy-two minutes.

   In explaining the discrepancy between the duration of *bein hashmashos* according to Rabbi Yehuda in *Shabbos* and Rabbi Yehuda in *Pesachim*, Rabbeinu Tam explains that there are two separate sunsets: Sunset I, which begins immediately after the sun has sunk below the horizon and lasts fifty-eight-and-a-half minutes, and Sunset II, which starts thereafter when light begins to fade into darkness and lasts an additional thirteen-and-a-half minutes until nightfall.

   According to Rabbeinu Tam, the period on Friday between Sunset I and Sunset II (fifty-eight-and-a-half minutes) is considered weekday, during which time all weekday work may be performed and one may light candles until Sunset II, i.e., fifty-eight-and-a-half minutes after Sunset I.

20    It is also of significant note that Chazal refer to the soul of a *talmid chacham* as Shabbos (*Zohar*, vol. 3, 29a). This is because Shabbos is the *tachlis*, or purpose, of creation and the Torah scholar is also the pinnacle or apex of what the world was created for.

# THE SHABBOS
# THE RABBI DREADED
# THE SERMON

dreaded the pulpit. I usually enjoy speaking, but not then. My charge as a rabbi is to bring strength and inspiration to my congregants. The problem is I'm not a politician. I couldn't fake the way I felt and I felt despondent and depressed. Hamas operatives had kidnapped three Israeli teenagers and the situation didn't look good.[21]

## NOT A GOOD TRACK RECORD

I thought of Nachshon Wachsman and Gilad Shalit. His Arab kidnappers

---

21    In the summer of 2014, Gilad Shaar, Eyal Yifrach and Naftali Fraenkel were kidnapped on their way home from school. After a frantic eighteen-day search, their bodies were discovered. The unity of Klal Yisrael in this trying time will not easily be forgotten.

killed Nachshon in a failed rescue attempt. Nachshon's death accented the difficulty even the most skilled soldiers would have in freeing the teenagers. On the other hand, Gilad Shalit sat imprisoned by Hamas for over five years. That situation is unfathomable for any human being, though complicated by the sacrifices made to ultimately bring Gilad Shalit home. There is a strong argument that such swaps dare not be repeated.[22] A real conundrum if I ever saw one.

## A FEMALE REBBI

So how was I to strike a hopeful tone with my congregants? The biggest problem for me was the directive from Rachel Fraenkel, mother of one of the kidnapped boys. All week, the entire world had been mesmerized by her passion in front of the media. Her dignity and strength under the most trying circumstances was the stuff legends are made of. In a call with the Rabbinical Council of America (RCA) immediately before Shabbos, she implored us to speak with our congregations on Shabbos about the boys. She requested we deliver a message of inspiration, of hope and of action.

There is a Talmudic principle of *"ein mesarvin bifnei gadol,"* that one cannot ignore or refuse the entreaty of a great person[23]—and this certainly qualified as such. I was *stuck* having to give the sermon, the one where if you do a good job and they metaphorically applaud, you respond that you wish events hadn't provided the opportunity to give such a stirring speech. The difficulty was confounded by my inability to hear or read almost anything uplifting or convincing regarding the *"matzav"* the entire week leading up to my sermon.

## DO YOU HAVE ENOUGH?

The *parshah* of *Korach* is primarily focused on a rebellion and on enmity and discord within our people. We are taught that Moshe scolds

---

22    Dovid Lichtenstein, in his book of halachic debates entitled *Headlines* (OU Press, 2014), has a piece on page 317 addressing the Shalit deal, in which he raises serious theoretical halachic issues with such an exchange, though does not actually *pasken* the *she'ilah*.

23    *Bava Metzia* 87a.

Korach with the message of "*Rav lachem bnei Levi*"[24]—It is enough for you to ascend to the *leviyah* and you shouldn't also pursue the *kehunah*. The Talmud teaches that Moshe was punished for scolding Korach in this fashion.[25] Later on, when Moshe yearns to enter the Land of Israel, Hashem tells Moshe in similar language, "*Rav Lach*—You have enough."[26]

The Manchester Rosh Yeshiva makes an astounding connection. He suggests that although Korach may have been misguided, he was still yearning on some level to reach a higher level of service to Hashem. Moshe seemingly wants to enter the Land of Israel so that he, too, can attain higher spiritual goals and focus, facilitated by additional commandments connected to the land. By using similar language in rebuking Moshe, G-d is reminding him that Korach is no different than he in seeking to reach a more intense spiritual connection. The parallel language of the Torah is loudly proclaiming that passion to rise spiritually must not be taken lightly. Even if misguided, it is a valiant, influential and noble attempt, and as such must be respected and not summarily dismissed with words such as "enough already."

> WHEN IT COMES TO MATTERS OF THE SPIRIT, THERE IS NO SUCH THING AS ENOUGH!

When it comes to matters of the spirit, there is no such thing as enough!

## A MESSAGE FROM BIBI NETANYAHU

These words, coupled with those of Rachel Fraenkel, gave me the temerity to attempt to shape a meaningful message. Mrs. Fraenkel shared words she heard directly from Prime Minister Netanyahu, about the serious concern that at a certain point in the army's search, there would be world pressure to relent or curtail the search. I communicated to my congregation the need to be proactive and stress the humanitarian aspects of the story, of boys being kidnapped on the way home from school. It

---

24     *Korach* 16:7.
25     *Sotah* 13b.
26     *Va'eschanan* 3:26.

struck me that a country such as the United States of America, that has repeatedly fallen victim to gun violence in schools, could connect with and empathize with the pain of teenagers taken at gunpoint upon returning home from school.

## TIMES SQUARE AND BILLBOARDS

I shared that I was particularly proud of an individual congregant.[27] The congregant called me on Friday with an idea as I hung up from the call with Rachel Fraenkel. He suggested renting out a billboard in Times Square to advertise the plight of the three boys and he solicited my help in making the idea come to fruition. After a few more calls, the wildly ambitious idea was en route to being actualized. I was inspired by the power and potential influence of the few and challenged my young *kehillah* to use their individual talents and creative energies to help the boys reach freedom.[28] After feeling helpless and despondent all week long, I began to see that maybe some small steps could be taken to bring attention and help to this horrible situation.

Parenthetically, the billboard garnered worldwide media attention. My friend, the former Governor of Hawaii, Linda Lingle,[29] reached out to me that she even heard about it in Hawaii. Subsequently, we at the Young Israel were again instrumental in orchestrating a similar public relations campaign for the Shabbos Project initiated by Rabbi Warren Goldstein, Chief Rabbi of South Africa.[30]

---

27    To give credit where it is due—my long-time congregant Yalli Hakalir thought of this brilliant idea.

28    Echoing the Chanukah theme of *"Rabim b'yad me'atim*—Many in the hands of the few," from the *Al Hanissim* prayer. At times, a little light can push away much darkness as Rabbi Yisrael Salanter is quoted to have said. In fact, the Lubavitcher Rebbe reminded Bibi Netanyahu of this exact adage before he embarked on the difficult task of acting as Israeli ambassador to the United Nations many years ago.

29    I met the governor at a Tikvah Fund seminar in New York City and remembered her as the individual who introduced vice presidential candidate Governor Sara Palin of Alaska at the 2008 Republican National Convention. I recall thinking at the time that Governor Lingle would have been a much better and more substantive choice for candidate John McCain.

30    This is a worldwide initiative to get as many Jews as possible to keep one entire Shabbos. It is usually designated for shortly after Sukkos.

## A NUCLEAR WEAPON

As Mrs. Fraenkel emphasized, the largest impact would ultimately be effectuated with spiritual weapons. Although I had been skeptical that we in America could make a significant contribution, it was hard not to listen and follow the directives of this Jewish mother. Her message was really similar to what G-d said to Moshe. We should never make light of spiritual yearnings because ultimately the world of the spirit is extremely powerful. People want to grow bigger spiritually because they realize their new persona and level can change realities on the ground.[31] When it comes to the power of spirituality to impact the world and possibly change events, we should never be skeptical or doubt. We have an extremely potent tool of unifying as a people in prayer and beseeching the heavens for a miraculous event. I was now telling the crowd (and convincing myself) to think Entebbe[32] rather than Wachsman or Shalit.

Ultimately, the message is to never give up on anybody. Certainly not to give up on the Creator of the Universe—Who can make anything happen in an instant. A valiant message, indeed, gleaned from my new mentor and teacher Mrs. Rachel Fraenkel.

## POSTSCRIPT

Sadly, we all know this story didn't end well. Yet, I often find myself drawing on those eighteen days and the strength exhibited by the three mothers as I move forward. Often in life, things appear dire and highly likely to have a negative ending. Still, it is so significant to remain as optimistic as possible while there is still the faintest of hope.[33] There will be

---

31    The Rambam in the *Laws of Teshuvah*, chap. 7, discusses how spiritual acts and true repentance can transform a person.

32    Operation Entebbe is the historic operation of the Israeli Defense Forces' Sayeret Matkal unit in 1976 to save approximately one hundred Jews who were being held in the Uganda airport by Palestinian terrorists.

33    Chazal teach in *Berachos* 10a that even with a sharp sword on your neck it is forbidden to relinquish hope for mercy.

ample time when things are over to mourn, scream and cry. However, there is also the important lesson of "It ain't over till it's over."[34] We must finish strong and then see where the cards fall, but not sabotage our best efforts in the interim.

Campaign in June 2014 to draw attention to the plight of three kidnapped Israeli boys. Eighteen days after searching and praying, Gilad, Eyal and Naftali were found near Chevron murdered by Hamas terrorists.

---

34     In Super Bowl 49, the Seattle Seahawks were one yard from scoring the winning touchdown with time running out. Incredibly, a rookie player made a marvelous interception and turned the game, and by extension the entire season, on its head. You just never know—it isn't over till it's over. This phrase was also popularized by baseball player Yogi Berra of the NY Yankees.

# SECTION TWO

## Family, Friends and Community

# MY SISTER-IN-LAW,
# MY HERO

hen I first met my future sister-in-law, I wouldn't have guessed that this young lady from Toronto would one day become my hero. Interestingly, our families went way back. My grandfather and hers were roommates in college and our fathers were classmates in high school. She made a nice impression and descended from significant and wonderful ancestry, but at that initial encounter, I would never have guessed the level of internal courage she possessed.

Tzivia was my parents' first daughter-in-law. She joined our clan of boys and we generally got along well. I remember her attempting to help me with *shidduchim* and ultimately how she shared words of encouragement the night before I got engaged to my wife. She brought joy to my parents by "delivering" their first grandchild (a beautiful baby girl) and she trailblazed for the other children-in-law who joined the family after her. Despite our appreciation for her, she was different from the rest of us. She grew up in a very large, tight-knit family, she had a funny accent and she wasn't afraid of blood. Let's just say the Cohen boys are a bit on the squeamish side.

So when, exactly, did Tzivia become my hero? It was during my phone call to her a week after she donated one of her kidneys to save a man's life. She explained to me the intricate details of the procedure that took place in a Tel Aviv hospital and how she was slowly recuperating. She concluded the conversation with the *brachah* of "*Im yirtzeh Hashem* by you," that I should merit a similar opportunity.

It wasn't a *brachah* that resonated with me, though I admired the sentiment and the passion of her convictions. What's marvelous about Tzivia isn't just that she is a busy mother of six, juggling her household responsibilities and a few part-time jobs to stay afloat in Israel. It's that this is the second life she has saved!

When she still lived in New York over ten years ago, she donated bone marrow and saved the life of a young boy living in Israel. I still remember the energy in the room when she was united with her recipient and his family at a gala dinner in a New York City hotel a year after the transplant. True to her unique style, Tzivia went the extra mile. She maintained a relationship with the recipient and his family and for many years, upon her *aliyah*, she drove to Afula to celebrate the recipient's birthday.

That was self-sacrifice for sure, but it didn't entail general anesthesia. It was also before Tzivia had a large family and many kids that relied upon her. When my brother called to share that Tzivia would be "doing it again," I was more than a little concerned. It wasn't my place to judge her choices... suffice it to say that I am more of a self-preservationist than she is. I would certainly try to save a person's life, but I'm pretty sure I wouldn't volunteer for the task.

We are taught that Hashem places before us the cure before the illness—"*hikdim refuah l'makah.*"[35] A few weeks prior to hearing about Tzivia's procedure, representatives of an amazing organization called Renewal spent a Shabbos on the Upper West Side and came to speak in my

---

35    *Megillah* 13b.

shul. We heard from donors and recipients about how their lives were changed through the giving/receiving experience. Interestingly, my parents were in the audience that weekend and also learned about kidney transplants. It sparked much conversation in the shul and I recall being asked theoretically by an earnest congregant if it's okay to take a kidney if you wouldn't be willing to donate one. Interesting question, no?

Little did we know that soon after this initial exposure, our family would be impacted by this complex topic, when Tzivia chose to save her second life. Thankfully, both Tzivia and her recipient have progressed nicely.

## GIVING GIFTS

An interesting postscript is what Tzivia said to me in the middle of our phone conversation after the procedure. She shared that her kidney recipient was a sixty-year-old non-religious man. Tzivia was already contemplating how she could bring him closer to Yiddishkeit. She wanted to give him a gift following his recuperation. Realizing that *tefillin* or a *sefer* were presumptuous and overstepping, she settled on a cup for washing hands, although she did confide that she hoped to somehow get an *Asher Yatzar* translation incorporated with the token gift.[36] This woman has an incorrigible desire to improve the lives of others—both physically and spiritually.

Many of us have ambitions to change the world for the better. Early in marriage, in our most idealistic phase, my wife and I would repeat a mantra that we aspired to be "big people." We meant that we hoped to impact and profoundly touch the lives of others. As I get older, I realize that it's a huge accomplishment just to touch the ones closest to us—and that is more than enough. With the challenges of marriage and raising kids, just living a simple life itself is not easy. Maybe we should just teach people

---

36     The special blessing we make upon leaving the bathroom, thanking G-d for our wondrous bodies and the various orifices we possess that help us dispose of waste products. It is found in the beginning of the *siddur* and placed in the preliminary blessings before the morning prayers.

to aspire toward being "small people" or "*pashuta Yidden*."[37] On the other hand, is that really what we should aim for?

I do carry a twinge of jealousy when I think of what my sister-in-law has done not once, but twice now. Any positive contribution that either of her recipients will make on the world going forward will be attributable to her selfless acts. The descendants of the boy she saved, any mitzvahs they may perform, can all be traced to her kindness. Through her pain, there has been tremendous gain. As our rabbis teach us, she has saved an entire world not once, but twice.[38] Despite my various *klal* efforts, it's hard to compare to our new family standard-bearer.

Of course, organ donation isn't for everyone. There are health restrictions and there are certainly risks and future concerns. That being said, it is becoming more widespread and is, of course, saving lives.

What the squeamish amongst us can do, at a minimum, is admire the Tzivias of the world and be inspired to greater kindness. If we won't give up a part of our "insides," we should be forthcoming with our "outsides," our bodies, to get them running toward goodness and *mitzvos*. There is plenty of risk-free activity that we can engage in to help others. We can cook a meal, give someone a ride or give someone a desperately needed hug or embrace. We can use the wondrous gift of a healthy body to effectuate all types of kindness. We can recite the *brachah* of *Asher Yatzar* with more fervor and intensity. We don't have to replicate Tzivia, rather we can be inspired by her message.

G-d has given each of us so much.

What can I give?

What can you give?[39]

---

37    This reminds me of my youngest son, Aharon, who always says, "I'm big, don't say that I'm little!" I try to explain that being little is also good. We don't always have to be so big in life!

38    *Sanhedrin* 37a.

39    I recently heard about another amazing gesture involving a kidney. Rabbi Larry Rothwachs, the rabbi of Congregation Beth Aaron in Teaneck, New Jersey, gave a kidney to save the life of Donny Hain, who is also a Teaneck resident. Donny is an individual with special needs, which makes the gesture even more meaningful as it validates that every single life is so precious no matter the capabilities or limitations of the person.

# WHERE EVERYBODY KNOWS YOUR NAME

There is a classic and catchy theme song from the successful television sitcom Cheers that includes the words, "Where everybody knows your name, and they're always glad you came... you want to go where everybody knows your name."[40] These lyrics poignantly describe a recent special Shabbos celebrated in the community where I grew up.

## HOME FOR SHABBOS AT LAST

It was my first Shabbos in my hometown of West Hempstead, New York in almost five years. My parents often visit us in Manhattan on weekends and we occasionally visit them on Sundays in their home as well. However, as a rabbi, Saturday is a "work day" and difficult to get away from my shul. On the occasional weekend off, for

---

40    This song was written by Gary Portnoy and Judy Hart Angelo.

various reasons, we have visited the place of my upbringing only sparingly. There is something very special about returning home. My mind was flooded with all different types of memories that were spurred by assorted locations in town. On Friday, I was a little hungry and took a drive past the ko-

**THERE IS SOMETHING VERY SPECIAL ABOUT RETURNING HOME.**

sher Carvel, Hunki's Pizza and the Chinese restaurant, Wing Wan. These were all places that I'd frequented hundreds of times in my youth, and I felt myself transported to a more carefree time in my life. I even ended up ordering pistachio ice cream with orange sorbet—the flavors I always used to enjoy, but hadn't had for many years.

## "YOU LOOK SO YOUNG AND CLEAN-SHAVEN!"

Friday afternoon, my daughter Anaelle was assigned to sleep in my old room while I was placed in a guest room for Shabbos. Anaelle found a portrait of me in my room from my law school graduation. I looked completely different and it was almost startling to her. I very much enjoyed sharing and explaining this piece of my past with her, as well as other vignettes that came up over the weekend. I also enjoyed looking over some of my old *sefarim* and other memorabilia.

## WHO IS THE CHILD?

Friday night, we came to the table for the Shabbos meal. I was supposed to sit in my old chair, immediately to the right of my father. My three-year-old son insisted on sitting in that seat. Surprisingly to me, I was a little disappointed. I always sat in that location and it was awkward for me to be sitting elsewhere. As soon as the opportunity presented itself, I moved back to my intended location. It had been a long time since I enjoyed my mother's meatballs, chicken soup and other delicacies. It felt just like old times, though I did miss the presence of my two younger brothers who live in Israel.

## SITTING WITH THE GOOD OLD BOYS CLUB

Shabbos morning was a real treat. I attended the 8:45 a.m. *minyan* and sat next to my father in my old seat in the main sanctuary. I was warmly greeted by many of my father's friends. Everybody had gotten a little older, a bit grayer, with expanded waistlines, but much was the same as well.

Some of these men have been sitting in the exact same seats for over forty years. The community has evolved and grown significantly from my childhood, but these men are still in their seats, carrying on the same conversations with their same friends. There is something very comfortable about things staying the same. It looked very similar to the 1980s when I grew up in the community. Although much has changed in their personal lives, the shul experience has remained a constant for them.

I will add that I'm very impressed that this entire group of men comes on time to shul. They may schmooze a bit during davening, but I've seen much worse behavior in other places. There is a modicum of maturity and respect that comes forth from this group of men I grew up watching. None of them would dare skip the rabbi's sermon and they are proud that they are back in time for it each week.

> SOME OF THESE MEN HAVE BEEN SITTING IN THE EXACT SAME SEATS FOR OVER FORTY YEARS.

## FAMILIARITY AND NACHAS

Having grown up with the children of many of these men, there is an amazing warmth and affection that is exhibited toward me. They feel a certain pride that I have become a rabbi, and that they "knew me when." The various banter and joking around over what to call me is also heartwarming. For this group, my first name is the only thing I think I'd ever be comfortable with.

> FOR THIS GROUP, MY FIRST NAME IS THE ONLY THING I THINK I'D EVER BE COMFORTABLE WITH.

It was also a treat that some of my childhood friends were visiting the neighborhood on this Shabbos. It probably has been at least twenty years since we all visited on the same weekend. Two of them currently live in Israel and it was a real joy to see them back in the old "hood." It must also be a *nachas* for the community to see what we have all gone on to accomplish in our unique fields.

> IT MUST ALSO BE A *NACHAS* FOR THE COMMUNITY TO SEE WHAT WE HAVE ALL GONE ON TO ACCOMPLISH IN OUR UNIQUE FIELDS.

## THE QUIET MASTERFUL ROLE MODEL

The most disappointing part of Shabbos was that the rabbi was away on vacation. Rabbi Yehuda Kelemer is one of my rabbinic heroes. West Hempstead has produced many *talmidei chachamim* and incredible contributors to the Jewish community over the years. Much of that success is due in no small part to Rabbi Kelemer's quiet demeanor and amazing presence as a role model for many of us as we grew up.

He was a bit of an enigma in certain ways. We didn't grow up in his home or have Shabbos meals with him, and I know he didn't sleep much, but he always exuded warmth, care and concern. He always had words that made us feel bigger than we actually were. Furthermore, Rabbi Kelemer also was a Torah giant. You just don't find that level of scholarship (and practical knowledge) much in the American rabbinate these days.

I didn't get to see or speak to Rabbi Kelemer often enough and it was disappointing to miss him on this visit. I had particularly enjoyed his overly effusive welcome last time I'd visited and I had to get along without the ego boost this time. Admittedly, as a rabbi on my own vacation, I certainly appreciated his time away as beneficial to him and his family, and definitely well deserved.

I did enjoy watching the new assistant rabbi, Rabbi Josh Goller, lead the community in his place. Rabbi Goller was a peer of my youngest brother and also grew up in our community. He exhibited a good sense of humor and much potential and dynamism. He certainly is fortunate to observe one of the masters of the trade up close and to help lead an amazing diverse community of various ages.

## WHERE HAS THE TIME GONE?

The most poignant part of the weekend was perusing the old albums. We snuck a peek at my bar mitzvah album and noticed a few interesting things. First, my daughter enjoyed seeing her current principal at Manhattan Day School, Rabbi Mordechai Besser, in attendance at my celebration. She didn't recognize him at all, but I explained that he was my principal when I was about her age and beyond.

It was sad to see how many people from the album were no longer amongst the living. I hold so many memories of these special people who contributed friendship to my family and look so vibrant and alive in those pictures. Thirty years have passed since that event and this sad feeling in reminiscing is of course to be expected.

> IT WAS SAD TO SEE HOW MANY PEOPLE FROM THE ALBUM WERE NO LONGER AMONGST THE LIVING.

## MY SPECIAL SPOT

Sunday morning, I went to *minyan* and then conversed with Dr. David Shatz, a renowned Jewish philosopher and friend of my family. He walked me to my home across the street from shul where we stood for a long while continuing the conversation. I was reminded of the many talks I had with friends in front of my parents' home about *shidduchim*, job opportunities, career paths and other things that I contemplated in my earlier days. Sure enough, when I finally came inside, my mother remarked that she remembered how that was "my spot."

## A BRIEF TOUR

I then decided to take a walk and invited my almost-eight-year-old daughter to join me. I took her to Halls pond where we had performed *tashlich* each year. As we walked around, I explained to her how the entire community would converge from different directions to attend. The best part was when she "tried out" a new park she discovered at the pond that she hoped to visit on her next trip to her grandparents' house.

I then took her to West Hempstead public high school for a walk around the track. I explained how I would often play tennis or basketball at this location, as she listened with interest. She also

SHE ALSO SHARED WITH ME THAT "YOU CAN'T TURN A CITY GIRL INTO A SUBURBAN GIRL."

shared with me that "you can't turn a city girl into a suburban girl." I just chuckled at her candor and insight.

My hometown, West Hempstead, is a unique place. It is primarily middle class and doesn't have any airs about it. It is a Torah-true community with good priorities, homey and comfortable. A great place to have grown up—and to stay connected to.

In truth, though, going home is something so very necessary for all of us. No matter how far we have traveled in life, it is crucial to remember our roots, where we come from. It is wonderful to share our past with our children, and, hopefully, enjoy the feeling of being welcomed home.

# HEARING THE SILENT CRY OF ANOTHER

**W**omen all over the world will light candles and recite the blessing *"L'hadlik ner shel Yom Tov—*To light the candle of the Festival" at the onset of Rosh Hashanah. This formulation is appropriate as Rosh Hashanah is a Festival, in most ways comparable to the other three Festivals, Pesach, Shavuos and Sukkos.

However, there is a distinction between Rosh Hashanah and the other Festivals. The other Festivals have a pilgrimage to the Temple in Jerusalem as their central act of observance. The Jew is commanded on these three occasions to attempt to "see" or get close to the Divine presence, what we refer to as *re'iyas Panim*.[41]

In contrast, the fundamental principle of Rosh Hashanah is *listening*—as manifested through the requirement to hear the *shofar* blow.

---

41    *Re'eh* 16, 16–17.

Why is Rosh Hashanah different from the other Festivals in this specific way, with this specific theme?

## YOM HAZIKARON

One other unique theme stands out regarding Rosh Hashanah. On the first day of Rosh Hashanah, we read about G-d remembering our matriarch Sarah by enabling her to conceive after being barren for many years.[42] The *haftorah* of the first day relates how Chana, a model of prayer, was also remembered and enabled to conceive.[43] Furthermore, our tradition teaches that our matriarch Rachel conceived on Rosh Hashanah as well.[44]

Why were these great women "redeemed" on Rosh Hashanah?

Is there a connection between their salvation and Rosh Hashanah's theme of listening?

## VALUE OF A LISTENING EAR

The Talmud discusses the law of an assailant who makes his victim deaf.[45] The conclusion is that the victim must be compensated his total pre-injury value on the slave market and not just the value of the ear. The Gaon of Vilna explains this ruling as being illustrative of the importance of the ability to hear.[46] Hearing, or the ability to listen, is connected to the deepest spiritual places within a person. A sophisticated and deep listener will be catapulted into knowledge of the depths of his fellow man. This vast potential to listen, understand and care is what makes each of us G-d-like and, by extension, of infinite

> HEARING, OR THE ABILITY TO LISTEN, IS CONNECTED TO THE DEEPEST SPIRITUAL PLACES WITHIN A PERSON.

---

42    *Vayera* 18:10.

43    *Shmuel I* 1:18.

44    *Rosh Hashanah* 11a.

45    *Bava Kama* 75b.

46    Quoted by Rabbi Bernard Weinberger in his *sefer Shemen HaTov* on the *moadim*, p. 52. He doesn't bring the *mareh makom* and I wasn't able to locate it. Much of this essay is informed by his piece.

worth. If a person's window into the soul of another is destroyed, his or her entire value must be compensated for. The ability to hear—and discern—is definitional to our being human.

There is an excellent book written by psychologist Michael Nichols entitled *The Lost Art of Listening*.[47] In the introduction, Nichols posits,

> Nothing hurts more than the sense that people close to us aren't really listening to what we have to say. We never outgrow the need to communicate what it feels like to live in our separate, private worlds of experience. That's why a sympathetic ear is such a powerful force in human relationships and why the failure to be heard and understood is so painful.[48]

These words echo the thought of the Gaon of Vilna in that they communicate and capture the essence of listening as a tool to reveal the depths of another. Attentive or focused listening is the process of gleaning the inner world of another and transmitting it into the inner recesses of oneself.

NOTHING HURTS MORE THAN THE SENSE THAT PEOPLE CLOSE TO US AREN'T REALLY LISTENING TO WHAT WE HAVE TO SAY.

## BEING CREATED ANEW

With this backdrop about the power of listening, we can now better grasp its centrality to Rosh Hashanah. Rosh Hashanah celebrates and commemorates the creation of man.[49] As the *shofar*-blower sounds the *shofar*, he is emulating G-d, Who breathed a breath of life—"*Va-yipach b'apav nishmas chayim*"—into the very first man.[50] On Rosh Hashanah, G-d judges us to determine if we are deserving of being "re-created" and granted another year of life. By using our power of listening (to the

---

47    *The Lost Art of Listening: How Learning to Listen Can Improve Relationships* (Guilford Press, 1996).

48    P. 1.

49    *Rosh Hashanah* 27a.

50    *Bereishis* 2:7. I heard this interpretation from Rabbi Moshe Shapiro.

*shofar*), we demonstrate that we understand this judgment process and we yearn to hear. Our attentiveness to the call of the *shofar* proclaims to G-d that, if re-created, we will connect to our fellow human beings and do our utmost to hear their cries. Even more—to penetrate their souls. With our lives hanging in the balance on Rosh Hashanah, it's not adequate just to see (as we do in the context of other Festivals), we must also *hear* and enable the sounds to penetrate and reverberate within us.

## THREE AMAZING WOMEN

This insight may shed light on the readings from the Torah and Prophets on the first day of Rosh Hashanah. Sarah, Rachel and Chana are invoked because the episodes surrounding their trials and tribulations involve hearing and feeling the pain of others.

The Torah juxtaposes G-d's remembering Sarah with the story of Avimelech. Avimelech captures Sarah and G-d punishes him with painful tribulations.[51] Avraham prays on behalf of Avimelech.[52] Ironically, his answered prayers ultimately expose him to the mockery of scoffers. They claim that Avimelech rather than Avraham impregnated Sarah.[53] Despite the repercussions, Avraham hears the anguish of Avimelech and prays on his behalf. In the merit of his selfless act, Hashem redeems Avraham as well, enabling him to father a child.[54]

G-d remembers Rachel because she heard the pain of her sister Leah and gave her the signs that she had established with Yaakov.[55] Chazal teach that Leah was destined to marry Esav, and Rachel was destined for Yaakov.[56] By divulging the signs, Rachel jeopardized her "claim" to Yaakov and became destined for Esav. She heard the cries of her sister and decided to endanger her own spiritual destiny to spare her sister the embarrassment of being rejected by Yaakov.

---

51     *Vayera* 20:18.
52     *Vayera* 20:17.
53     Rashi, *Toldos* 25:19.
54     *Bava Kama* 92a. Hashem answers his prayers and redeems him first.
55     Rashi, *Vayeitzei* 29:25.
56     Rashi, *Vayeitzei* 29:17.

Chana also, despite great personal suffering yearning for a precious child for so many years, is also willing to put her personal needs aside. Chana intuits or hears Hashem asking something of her, to offer her precious son to Him, and she offers the son that she so desperately coveted as an offering to Hashem. Apparently, Chana's cries for a child are embedded more in her deep will to serve Hashem then they are to fulfill a personal need.

In all three episodes, the trait of selflessness led to a Rosh Hashanah redemption. This is no coincidence. Redemption occurs on Rosh Hashanah, a day of listening, for those selfless individuals who hear the cries and pain of others and understand that they were created to reach beyond themselves.

## A HIDDEN PRAYER

These insights also shed light on another Rosh Hashanah anomaly. The days of the holiday are intensive days of prayer, invoking themes of *malchuyos*, *zichronos* and *shofaros*.[57] We then go home in the evenings[58] and eat various foods that symbolize requests for a fruitful year.[59] Why is this necessary? Were our intensive prayers in the daytime somehow inadequate? It is explained that during the day we pray for the collective, the well-being of the entire world. At night, when things are dark, we go home and *hint* to G-d about our own needs as well, but our first priority is other people.

---

57    *Rosh Hashanah* 32a.
58    There are different sources and practices as to whether the *simanim* are done on both nights of Rosh Hashanah or just the initial evening.
59    *Kerisus* 6a.

# MORE THAN MEETS THE EYE

s the father of a special-needs child, I'm often sensitive to the way people view my son: Will they judge him by his disabilities? Or will they be able to see past his challenges and appreciate the beautiful child that he is?

You can then only imagine my joy one summer upon walking the streets of Jerusalem with my son and hearing the accolades bestowed upon him. Numerous times, absolute strangers would approach us and proclaim, "*Tzaddik!*" (righteous one). This label would often be followed up with an explanation of my son's tremendous spiritual virtues and how fortunate we were to have him in our family.

## BONDING AND COMING TOGETHER

This uplifting experience accompanied me into the *Yamim Noraim* period. It caught my attention that our prayers on Rosh Hashanah are very focused on mankind at large. We are repeatedly beseeching G-d that all the nations of the world become a single society.[60] We yearn for the days when G-d will be accepted as king over the entire corpus of creation.

The entire mankind should unite? Middle East peace, Jews and Muslims, Iran all coming together? Pretty ambitious—or, shall I say, audacious—prayers that we are offering up. Are we so unified as Jews that we are ready to move on to more global issues?

My summer experience notwithstanding, do we really respect, support and love our brothers and sisters of diverse outlooks?

MY SUMMER EXPERIENCE NOTWITHSTANDING, DO WE REALLY RESPECT, SUPPORT AND LOVE OUR BROTHERS AND SISTERS OF DIVERSE OUTLOOKS?

## TEMPLES AND DESTRUCTION

The Talmud teaches us that the first Temple was destroyed because the Jewish people violated the three cardinal sins for which we are directed to give our lives rather than violate them (idol worship, bloodshed and immorality).

The second Temple's destruction is attributed to baseless hatred amongst ourselves.[61]

The contrast is striking. The cardinal sins, the worst the Torah speaks of, are seemingly being put on par with baseless hatred or lack of consideration of another person's feelings. Why is mere insensitivity—as bad as it is—placed on par with the worst of sins?

WHY IS MERE INSENSITIVITY—AS BAD AS IT IS—PLACED ON PAR WITH THE WORST OF SINS?

## THE FINAL/PARTING WORDS

The answer is in the *Shema* prayer. We speak daily of the oneness of

---

60  We mention in the *amidah* of *Mussaf* that all creations should become an *agudah achas*, bound together as one in service of Hashem. We also pray for rejoicing in the holy land—"*simchah l'artzecha, v'sasson l'irecha*," which will come from world peace, and also that Hashem should rule over all of creation—"*al kol ma'asecha*."

61  *Yoma* 9b.

G-d.[62] The word *"echad,"* one, is the last word recited by every Jew. This word reverberates throughout Jewish history as the final cry of the soul departing its earthly abode.[63] We are declaring at such critical moments (as well as daily) that G-d, who is one, is therefore most comfortable in the environs of unity and consequently chooses to reside in places of oneness.

> THE WORD *"ECHAD,"* ONE, IS THE LAST WORD RECITED BY EVERY JEW. THIS WORD REVERBERATES THROUGHOUT JEWISH HISTORY AS THE FINAL CRY OF THE SOUL DEPARTING ITS EARTHLY ABODE.

The holy Temple, G-d's sanctuary on earth, must manifest oneness. A Temple cannot continue to exist upon a foundation of discord and enmity. That is why Aharon Hakohen (whose modus operandi in life is making peace, creating unity among people)[64] is designated as the supervisor of the service in the Mishkan, the predecessor of the Temple. He embodies the unity necessary for G-d to dwell amongst us. Aharon also visits us in the *sukkah* as he embodies our hope for G-d's canopy of peace that we desperately yearn for.[65] He also links us to world peace and the more universalistic aspects alluded to throughout the Sukkos Festival.

## CAN WE ALL JUST GET ALONG?

We talk a lot about world peace on Rosh Hashanah, and allude to this theme again throughout Sukkos.[66] Indeed, it is a running theme throughout all of Judaism and all of Jewish life.

G-d is demanding something from us. The broader, more global issues are in His hands. He wants us to take care of business at home and

> THE BROADER, MORE GLOBAL ISSUES ARE IN HIS HANDS.

---

62    *"Shema Yisrael Hashem Elokeinu Hashem Echad*—Hear O Israel Hashem is our G-d and He is One."

63    It is the central component of the *Vidui* a person recites on his deathbed. It is interestingly also recited at the end of Yom Kippur, which is a resurrection of sorts of spiritually returning from death to life and hopefully a good new year.

64    *Avos* 1:12.

65    He is one of the seven *ushpizin*, the special guests we invite into the *sukkah*.

66    We ask in our prayers and in *bentching* that Hashem rebuild the *Sukkas Dovid*, the holy Temple, which will usher in a period of revelation and world peace.

then He will be inspired to bring about the broader world peace that we so fervently aspire to.

## LOOK A LITTLE DEEPER

For G-d's presence to permeate our lives and communities, He demands of us a commitment to unity and love for each other.

> FOR G-D'S PRESENCE TO PERMEATE OUR LIVES AND COMMUNITIES, HE DEMANDS OF US A COMMITMENT TO UNITY AND LOVE FOR EACH OTHER.

*A young man was in line to visit the famed Skverer Rebbe of New Square, NY. He was wearing jeans, a polo shirt and a kippah srugah. He was eyed suspiciously by the gabbai, as his garb was not the norm. Upon entry to the Rebbe he asked for a brachah for a refuah shleimah for Dovid ben Sara. The gabbai overheard the request and asked the young man what his connection was to Dovid ben Sara. The young man explained that he was a counselor in Camp HASC for special-needs children and that Dovid ben Sara was his camper. It was the boy's birthday and he thought it would be a meaningful gift to receive a brachah from the boy's Rebbe, as the boy's family were Skverer chassidim. The gabbai began to cry uncontrollably. The young man apologized and asked the gabbai why he was crying. The gabbai replied, "Dovid ben Sara is my son and I'm incredibly moved by your efforts on his behalf."*

G-d wants us to get past the externals and assumptions about one another and dig deeper to find the really good stuff.

Each of us is special, unique and beautiful. Our job is to see it in others—and ourselves.

# WHAT'S YOUR NAME?

I was once flying on an airplane and met an elderly gentleman who knew my grandfather, Rabbi Meir Felman, from their days in yeshiva. He shared that my grandfather, coming from a small, unheralded town, didn't have a "name" coming into the yeshiva. However, when he left the yeshiva, everyone knew who he was. It is rare for me to meet acquaintances of my grandfather and I left the airplane more than a little proud.[67]

## REPUTATION OR "STREET CRED"

People often contemplate how to make a "name for themselves." Whether in the rabbinate or other professional endeavors, many of us covet a certain level of recognition

MANY OF US COVET A CERTAIN LEVEL OF RECOGNITION OR OUTER ACKNOWLEDGMENT OF OUR TALENTS AND PROWESS.

---

67    I once spoke in Los Angeles and mentioned my grandfather. A man approached after my lecture and said that my grandfather was his *mesader kiddushin* and he subsequently emailed me various pictures and other mementos from the synagogue in which my grandfather served as rabbi. It was a real special treat for me and I forwarded the material on to my entire extended family to much amazement and excitement.

or outer acknowledgment of our talents and prowess. Ideally, we mostly focus on our own perceptions of how we are doing, but rare is the person who doesn't pay attention at all to what other people think.

Chazal teach about running from honor versus running toward honor.[68] It is a delicate balance to desire a little recognition but not fully pursue honor; to approach this dichotomy deftly, not making life all about honor and glory, while also not being completely irreverent.

## INSPIRATION FROM CHICAGO

I'm not a *chassid* of President Obama by any stretch, but I did come across this meaningful quote from him. In response to a query as to when he felt most broken in his life, he gave the following insightful answer:

> I first ran for Congress in 1999, and I got beat. I just got whooped. I had been in the state legislature for a long time, I was in the minority party, I wasn't getting a lot done, and I was away from my family and putting a lot of strain on Michelle. Then for me to run and lose that bad, I was thinking maybe this isn't what I was cut out to do. I was forty years old, and I'd invested a lot of time and effort into something that didn't seem to be working. But the thing that got me through that moment, and any other time that I've felt stuck, is to remind myself that it's about the work. Because if you're worrying about yourself—if you're thinking: Am I succeeding? Am I in the right position? Am I being appreciated?—then you're going to end up feeling frustrated and stuck. But if you can keep it about the work, you'll always have a path. There's always something to be done.[69]

Part of focusing on the task at hand is realizing that we are ideally assessed by the sum total of our actions. Therefore, each and every action

---

68      *Avos* 1:13.

69      Amazingly, just a few years later he was a US Senator and then President of the United States. He shared this in an interview conducted in the Oval Office with a reporter.

deserves focus and effort, but only because it is significant in creating an overall tapestry.[70] A beautiful parable for this idea is that when you flip a coin, as it floats in the air sometimes it is heads and sometimes tails. What matters most is

> PART OF FOCUSING ON THE TASK AT HAND IS REALIZING THAT WE ARE IDEALLY ASSESSED BY THE SUM TOTAL OF OUR ACTIONS.

how it lands, not the intermediary stuff.[71] The intermediate state is the process, but also just one point in a progression.

## IS PERCEPTION REALITY?

Often, due to this progression and the continuum in which we live, in attempting to describe a person, we struggle to define his essence, the core basis of his being. A person can have many fine characteristics, but ultimately his reputation is the sum total of those various traits. Perception is reality. Our reputations and how others perceive us tend to define to the world—and often to ourselves—who we really are.

We are taught in *Pirkei Avos* that there are three Jewish crowns—the crown of Torah, the crown of priesthood and the crown of kingship. We are then instructed that a fourth crown supersedes the other three: the crown of a good name.[72]

What is the source for this teaching? It is rooted in a *midrash* on Koheles.[73] The verse in Koheles teaches: "*Tov shem mi-shemen tov*—A good name trumps the inaugural oils of the *kohen* or king." The *midrash* elaborates on this point through an example: Nadav and Avihu, who possessed

---

70    Post Super Bowl 49, I read two contrasting analyses about two football players on different sides of the pendulum. One was about how the Green Bay Packers cut Brandon Bostick from the team after he botched an on-side kick at the end of the NFC championship game, directly resulting in their missing the Super Bowl. In the big game itself, Malcolm Butler, a rookie for the Patriots made a historic game-saving goal-line interception with the clock running out. Both players said afterwards, they don't want to be remembered for just one play, good or bad. What a terrific message that no matter how high or how low we are, it is just one moment on a given trajectory.

71    Rabbi Hutner, in his *Igros U'ketavim*, letter #128 to a struggling student, formulates this challenge as "losing the battle but winning the war."

72    *Avos* 4:17.

73    *Koheles Rabbah* 7:1.

Torah and *kehunah*, the "*shemen tov*," entered a place of life, the Holy of Holies, and ultimately died there; whereas Chananel, Mishael and Azaryah, possessing only their good names, entered a fiery furnace—a place of death—and came out unscathed.

The crowning glory of a stellar reputation trumps other positions and accolades.

## CROWNS OF GLORY–THREE PLUS ONE

The Rambam describes the three initial crowns (Torah, priesthood and kingship) as the three qualities that distinguish our people.[74] This point is illustrated in the context of our being adorned with the crown of Torah at Har Sinai when Hashem specifically refers to us as being a *mamleches kohanim*, a kingdom of priests.[75] The three crowns are therefore very much intertwined.

We are actually introduced to this concept earlier in *Pirkei Avos*. The introductory chapter posits that the world stands on three things: Torah, *avodah* (service) and *chesed* (kindness).[76] Torah is G-d's ultimate gift to His people; *avodah* encapsulates the role of the *kohanim* in the Temple; and kindness is the ultimate kingly trait since with special privilege comes unique responsibility to others. So here too, we observe the three juxtaposed and presented together, this time as foundational to the world's existence.

It is most confounding, then, that despite the life-altering significance of the three crowns (indeed, the world stands on them—and exists for them!), the later *mishnah* tells us of a loftier fourth crown. The *mishnah* might be saying that while there are three equally significant crowns, there is one crown, that of a *shem tov*, that climbs on the back ("*oleh al gabeihen*") of the other three; i.e., if one has the three specific qualities or crowns, what emanates from them is a *shem tov*. The whole is greater than the sum of its parts.[77]

---

74    *Peirush Hamishnah.*
75    *Yisro* 19:6.
76    *Avos* 1:2.
77    Aristotle.

## WATCH YOUR BACK

This approach can be understood when one reflects on the role of the *gabbai* in a synagogue. *Gabbai* has the word *"gav,"* back, as its root and communicates that the individual has the back (as in "I've got your back") of the shul and the rabbi; he supports and looks after both of them.[78]

I have a good friend who does something unique every year during the *Yamim Noraim* when he gets to the part in the *Mussaf* liturgy about giving a crown to Hashem.[79] He gesticulates the placement of an imaginary crown on an imaginary head.[80] This is his way of concretizing the process of the ultimate coronation in the New Year. It also illustrates what we all should be striving for—we'd ideally like to be crowned with a *shem tov* and have it publicly displayed for all to see. The aggregate of our efforts in Torah, *avodah* and *chesed* is the positive name that emanates directly from them.

> THE AGGREGATE OF OUR EFFORTS IN TORAH, *AVODAH* AND *CHESED* IS THE POSITIVE NAME THAT EMANATES DIRECTLY FROM THEM.

We can create our names or reputations, but sometimes we get a head start. Our given personal or family name can carry a certain heft.

## THE WEIGHT OF A NAME

A good family name or personal name after a *tzaddik* is also a burden or a heavy weight to bear. A good name is sometimes passed down to the next generation, which then must struggle to preserve it and not be crushed by its expectations. In fact, there is a prominent rabbinic family I know in which the mother used to tell her children upon their leaving the house, "Don't forget that

> A GOOD FAMILY NAME OR PERSONAL NAME AFTER A *TZADDIK* IS ALSO A BURDEN OR A HEAVY WEIGHT TO BEAR.

---

78    This idea was shared with me by Rabbi Motty Katz, chaplain at NYU medical center when he served as my *gabbai* for a number of years.

79    In the *Mussaf* we say, *"V'yitnu lecha keser meluchah,"* that all the nations will join together and crown Hashem.

80    Rabbi Eli Reich, *Ram* at Yeshivat Sha'alvim.

you are a descendant of so-and-so." The desire was to motivate the children to live up to and not sell short such a rich legacy.

This idea is illustrated through the following anecdote.[81]

> *There is a philanthropist in Vienna named Thomas Moskowitz. He is the CEO of Bank Winter, which has assets in the billions of euros. He's not a man who accepts recognition so easily but a few years back he agreed to come to New Jersey to be honored in Lakewood.*
>
> *He began his remarks that evening by proclaiming, "I'm something really special." He went on to explain that the key to his success in business—and ultimately that of any businessman—is great timing. Those in attendance were shocked that he would speak so brashly of his prowess. He then dropped the punch line, explaining that he had wonderful timing in the sense that he succeeded his father, Simon Moskowitz, who founded the bank and set it on its successful course. The crowd chuckled, understanding (now) that he was actually a very humble person. He felt that his task was to preserve his family's good name.*

Each of us is given a specific name at birth, personal and familial. With those names come both potential and challenge. Our opportunity as we pass through this world is to meet that challenge and actualize that potential by engaging with the three crowns of glory and ensuring that a beautiful *shem tov* emanates from our efforts, thereby ensuring and confirming the validity and veracity of our given names and/or creating a new name for ourselves.

---

81    I heard this story listening to a *shiur* of my friend Rabbi Yehoshua Hartman of London and author of many *sefarim* on the Maharal of Prague.

# EUROPEAN
# ANTI-SEMITISM:
## MY WIFE IN HER OWN WORDS

have always had a special connection to my hometown. To most people, Vienna, Austria evokes images of anti-Semitism and the Holocaust. To me it was and still is one the most beautiful cities and the backdrop to all my fondest childhood memories. Vienna is the place where I grew up. It is where my aunt lives across the street and my grandmother lived down the block and where school is just a tram ride away. It is where I went for walks in the city center, sat in trendy coffee shops with friends and went ice skating in the winter. Vienna was home.

## EXILED

When I reached high school age, my parents decided that it was important for me to receive a strong Jewish education and to be in a more religious environment. Consequently, I attended high school in the United States and boarded with family. At this point, Vienna took on even greater significance to me. The highlight of my year was not only seeing my family but also coming back to Vienna and seeing them in familiar surroundings. Being in my apartment, davening in my father's shul, but also just walking down the familiar streets; these were all integral parts of the experience. It was something I couldn't explain. I knew I would not want to raise my own children there, and of course Vienna did not compare in terms of the *kedushah* of Eretz Yisrael.

And yet, there was nothing like Vienna, nothing like home—and the two were intrinsically connected. This strong bond continued for years, even after I got married. My husband would marvel that it did not matter how many times my parents visited us; it did not count until we had taken our yearly trip home to Vienna.

I am often asked about the existence of anti-Semitism in Austria. I usually reply that it is definitely an issue of concern but it is not something I have ever experienced personally. Never, that is, until a recent Pesach.

## PASSPORT CONTROL

It all began pretty innocently. My husband, son and I had just gotten off the plane from Tel Aviv and were standing in line at passport inspection. I was excited to be home again and was already making plans for the upcoming days. Suddenly I noticed that I had forgotten to bring my Austrian passport, but decided that it was not important as I could enter on my American one, like my husband and son.

We got to the front of the line and I handed the customs officer our passports, politely smiling and wishing her a good afternoon in German. She did not smile back and harshly told me that she only accepts one passport at a time. I was a little taken aback but tried to comply with her demands. She, however, was determined to make things difficult for us. She would not accept my husband's passport unless he handed it to her instead of me but when he moved forward to give it to her, she snapped that she had to stamp the baby's first and warned us that we might "have a problem" soon.

My husband does not understand German so he could not follow our interaction, but he clearly understood what was going on. It did not really matter what the woman said, her tone of voice and attitude spoke louder than words.

The whole incident only took about three minutes and the exact details are not important. When it was over and we moved on to claim our luggage, I burst into tears.

I was outraged. Never in my life had I been treated like this. Didn't this woman know who I was? I was the daughter of the Chief Rabbi of Austria! I was an Austrian citizen! I was... a Jew! The realization hit me like a brick. Though the word "Jew" had not come up in our little altercation, it was clear that the customs officer had not particularly liked my husband's *kippah* or my *sheitel*.

> IT DID NOT REALLY MATTER WHAT THE WOMAN SAID, HER TONE OF VOICE AND ATTITUDE SPOKE LOUDER THAN WORDS.

## REALITY SINKING IN

While we were waiting for our luggage, I was still fuming. Who was this woman anyway? I was going to get her fired. How dare she make me feel like a foreigner in my own home! How dare she make me feel so helpless and wronged! It would be hard to prove, though, that her motivations had been anti-Semitic. Maybe she was just having a very bad day. And one might argue that it was her prerogative to demand that the passports be given to her in a certain order.

> HOW DARE SHE MAKE ME FEEL LIKE A FOREIGNER IN MY OWN HOME! HOW DARE SHE MAKE ME FEEL SO HELPLESS AND WRONGED!

After calming down a bit and giving it some more thought, I decided not to pursue the matter. This incident would not really make a difference in the grand scheme of things. And I did not even know this woman's name. My American husband who doesn't expect much better from the Austrians, the perpetrators of the Holocaust, was much less disturbed than I was. I, on the other hand, was and still am shaken up. For me, this incident has had greater significance. My perfect vision of Vienna has been shattered.

## HOME REDEFINED

No matter how I feel about Vienna, my visits may not be as enthusiastically received as I would like them to be. I may know every side street but that doesn't mean I can walk down them undisturbed.

The truth of the matter is that Vienna will always be my childhood home. The warm associations and connections I have established cannot be erased so easily. But now, every time I come back "home" and stand in line at passport inspection, I have a built-in subtle reminder not to get too carried away. I have learned that home is not only where the heart is, it is also a place where you are wanted.

> I HAVE LEARNED THAT HOME IS NOT ONLY WHERE THE HEART IS, IT IS ALSO A PLACE WHERE YOU ARE WANTED.

Photo of Judea Center, the shul in Brooklyn that my maternal grandfather, Rabbi Meir Felman, presided over for many years. He was instrumental in the ultimate sale of the building and ensuring the proceeds made their way to various institutions in Eretz Yisroel including his "baby" Mevaseret Zion. The yeshiva Mevaseret continues to carry on it the name Judea Center to this very day.

Photo of my grandfather meeting with revered Prime Minister of Israel Menachem Begin.

# SECTION THREE

Lessons in Parenting

from the Father of a

Special-Needs Child

# ONE STEP AT A TIME: A SPECIAL-NEEDS ODYSSEY

I t had to be HaRav Moshe Shapiro.

When I contemplated whom to honor as *sandak* for our newborn son with Down syndrome, R' Moshe was the obvious choice. It wasn't just because I desired a great and distinguished *rav* for the role, but because he had demonstrated sensitivity to our specific plight.

When you are told that your *bechor* will have a life-long cognitive disability, you grasp onto whatever you can for *chizuk*. For me, it was a *mazel-tov* letter written years earlier by R' Moshe to Rabbi Baruch Rabinowitz, celebrating the recent birth of a child with Down syndrome named Nota Shlomo.[82]

---

82    A special thank you to my dear friend Aaron Kinderlehrer for providing me a copy of this

## A PROFOUND LETTER OF COMFORT

R' Moshe wrote that Nota Shlomo was a "wonderful gift," a gift with the potential to transform the lives of his parents and bring forth well-springs of love from the depths of their hearts. He also alluded to how the elevated soul of such a child is sent to this world not for its own sake, but rather to help those around it.

I would be lying if I told you this line of reasoning was comforting at the time of my sons's birth. But what I did find comforting was the message that every little step Nota Shlomo would advance in terms of attaining human dignity, deductive reasoning and developing independence would be considered an accomplishment equivalent to conquering an entire world. R' Moshe even commented that "*halevai*" everybody understood this most fundamental principle of Yiddishkeit. This insight, coupled with the palpable love and concern expressed by R' Moshe for his beloved but anguished *talmid* years ago, made him the clear choice to be our *sandak*.

> I WOULD BE LYING IF I TOLD YOU THIS LINE OF REASONING WAS COMFORTING AT THE TIME OF MY SONS'S BIRTH.

## ZEH HAKATAN GADOL YEHIYEH

letter at that critical time. Aaron is a kindred spirit and served as the Chairman of the Board of Yachad for many years. See appendix 1 for the Hebrew version of the letter.

Now, years later, two things still stand out about the *bris* of our Ye-didya Shlomo. The first was the embrace R' Moshe gave me when he arrived at the *simchah*, and his comment, "I *promise* you he will be a typical child." The second was R' Moshe accenting and highlighting Yedidya's immense potential by proclaiming quite loudly "*gadol*" when my Rosh Yeshiva, Rabbi Yaakov Friedman, read the words "*Zeh ha-katan gadol yehiyeh*" during the *kerias ha-shem*.

In my office, I have a big picture of R' Moshe with baby Yedidya Shlomo on his lap at the *bris*. I often look at the

I OFTEN LOOK AT THE PHOTO, AND IT BRINGS ME BACK TO A DIFFERENT TIME IN MY LIFE.

photo, and it brings me back to a different time in my life. I remember the trepidation, the tears, the questions and the search for comfort.

Rav Moshe Shapiro serving as *sandak* at the *bris* of Yedidya Shlomo Cohen at Yeshivas Birchas Mordechai in Har Nof, Jerusalem, July 2005.

I realize now that sometimes in life, you just have to flow with a situation, and resolution just comes by itself at some later point. There's never any great epiphany, it just somehow becomes okay—and even normal—with the passage of time. It is like what I once heard a *mesader kiddushin* say under the *chuppah* of an older single who finally married a girl he had dated years earlier, "*Mah shelo yaaseh ha-sechel yaaseh ha-zman*—What intelligence doesn't accomplish, time will."[83]

## WHAT IS TYPICAL ANYWAY?

The beauty is that R' Moshe's *brachah* has come true.

I'll admit that when he "promised" Yedidya would be a typical child, I wishfully thought that he was predicting that he would genuinely be "regular" or even "cured." But while Yedidya still has Down syndrome, he is certainly typical of other children—which is, of course, what R' Moshe meant.

It is a great *nachas* to watch Yedidya come to understand and apply concepts that he gleans from his environment. It is a great joy to us, even when his formulations of certain terms or expressions are less than perfect. He enthusiastically calls *shabbatonim* that he participates in a "*shabbos-a-tone*," and often inquires when the next one will be.[84] Yet, he clearly is excited and understands that this is a unique weekend away from home exclusively for him. As R' Moshe said in his letter, an iota of deductive reasoning, "*meivin davar mi-toch davar*," is to capture an entire world.

Once, Yedidya's amazing *rebbi*, Rabbi Yehoshua Fulda of Washington Heights,[85] asked to speak with me. He shared how often Yedidya will intentionally answer wrongly to a question in a most playful manner. Rabbi Fulda was proud of this chicanery and cunning. It shows him that Yedidya is "typical," since he obviously knows the correct answer, but wants to keep his *rebbi* on his toes. Rabbi Fulda also shared, with tears in his eyes, that he has never seen such an intense bond between father and

---

83    Rabbi Kenneth Hain of Beth Sholom in Lawrence, New York. The situation was a couple that dated and broke up because the boy wasn't yet ready. The woman married someone else, divorced and ultimately returned to the original man whom she had dated. Ten years had elapsed since the first go-around. Thankfully, the man was now "ready" and they are happily married with children. Rabbi Hain was poking fun at the *chassan*, with whom he was very close, and got a great reaction from the crowd.

84    Yachad deserves great credit for the junior *shabbatonim* that they frequently run throughout the New York metropolitan area and across the country.

85    Rabbi Fulda always goes beyond the call of duty and is beloved to us as well as to the entire Upper West Side community. He learns with many students who have some sort of learning disability and makes a profound impact with his patient and diligent style—and funny ties.

son. I can't vouch for the veracity of his statement, but I was touched that the wellsprings of love that R' Moshe spoke of in his letter are palpable and apparent to a regular observer.

## ACCEPTING OR REJECTING CHALLENGES

A few years ago, a family we were acquainted with didn't take their baby home from the hospital because the baby had Down syndrome. It took much time and *chizuk* until we were able to convince them to take ownership of the child that Hashem gave them. I even understand that in some extremely rare circumstances, it could be beneficial to have someone else adopt the child. Obviously, this depends on the level of challenge coupled with the ability of the parents. However, such a weighty decision raises the very significant philosophical issue of whether or not Hashem "mistakenly" gifted this child to this couple. Does Hashem really make mistakes?

There are tremendous opportunities hidden in these challenges. There seems to be a proliferation of diagnoses in the world today; many children have some sort of unique disposition—behavioral or otherwise. Our task as parents is ultimately just to move our own child, whether "typical" or "special," to the next rung on their ladder. If we focus intently on this goal alone, we have done a service not just for our child, but also for the world at large.

> OUR TASK AS PARENTS IS ULTIMATELY JUST TO MOVE OUR OWN CHILD, WHETHER "TYPICAL" OR "SPECIAL," TO THE NEXT RUNG ON THEIR LADDER.

## GRADUATING

My family has a strong focus on education and academic achievement. I was accepted to an Ivy League college and graduated from a top-five Ivy League law school.

My Yedidya probably will not collect those degrees, but he can accomplish degrees of even greater significance. He will earn the degrees of *simchah*, *nachas* and self-esteem, helped by parents who understand fully what their *tafkid* is with their unique child.

In our uber-complex, technologically sophisticated society, there is something so refreshing, almost jarring, about the simplicity and purity of the special emissaries that Hashem surrounds us with. He sends them to re-orient us, inspire us and help us grow. Will we?

My son Yedidya Shlomo davening at the Kotel and standing on the field of MetLife Stadium at a Meor fundraiser and also the site of the Siyum Hashas.

# A VISIT TO HOLLAND IN REAL TIME

ne summer, my wife and I left our children in Vienna with my in-laws and headed off for a two-day getaway in Amsterdam. As we walked the cobblestoned streets, we marveled at the irony. After years of acclimating to metaphorical Holland, we were actually taking a breather from Holland in Amsterdam.

> AFTER YEARS OF ACCLIMATING TO METAPHORICAL HOLLAND, WE WERE ACTUALLY TAKING A BREATHER FROM HOLLAND IN AMSTERDAM.

What do I mean? Our oldest child, Yedidya, was born with Down syndrome in a Jerusalem hospital. The very next day, a midwife in the hospital[86] handed us a copy of "Welcome to Holland" by Emily Perl Kingsley.[87] She writes:

---

86    Interestingly, the midwife was the sister of my Rosh Yeshiva, Rabbi Yaakov Friedman. She also had a son with Down syndrome and walked us through our new situation with some tough love.

87    "Welcome to Holland" is an essay written in 1987 by Emily Perl Kingsley about having a child with a disability. The piece is given by many organizations to new parents of children with special needs.

I am often asked to describe the experience of raising a child with a disability—to try to help people who have not shared that unique experience to understand it, to imagine how it would feel. It's like this: When you're going to have a baby, it's like planning a fabulous vacation trip to Italy. You buy a bunch of guidebooks and make your wonderful plans. The Colosseum, the Michelangelo David, the gondolas in Venice. You may learn some handy phrases in Italian. It's all very exciting.

After months of eager anticipation, the day finally arrives. You pack your bags and off you go. Several hours later, the plane lands. The stewardess comes in and says, "Welcome to Holland."

"Holland?" you say. "What do you mean Holland? I signed up for Italy! I'm supposed to be in Italy. All my life I've dreamed of going to Italy."

But there's been a change in the flight plan. They've landed in Holland and there you must stay.

The important thing is that they haven't taken you to a horrible, disgusting, filthy place, full of pestilence, famine and disease. It's just a different place.

So you must go out and buy new guidebooks. And you must learn a whole new language. And you will meet a whole new group of people you would never have met.

It's just a different place. It's slower-paced than Italy, less flashy than Italy. But after you've been there for a while and you catch your breath, you look around... and you begin to notice that Holland has windmills... and Holland has tulips. Holland even has Rembrandts.

But everyone you know is busy coming and going from Italy... and they're all bragging about what a wonderful time they had there. And for the rest of your life, you will say, "Yes, that's where I was supposed to go. That's what I had planned."

And the pain of that will never, ever, ever, ever go away... because the loss of that dream is a very, very significant loss.

But... if you spend your life mourning the fact that you didn't get to Italy, you may never be free to enjoy the very special, the very lovely things... about Holland.

There is a linguistic challenge in the Torah relating to the Mishkan, G-d's Sanctuary. The verse says: *"V'yikchu Li terumah*—Take for Me a gift."[88] The Torah should have said it simply: *"V'yitnu*—give" a gift.

Perhaps the Torah is hinting at a novel idea. Whether giving or taking, a gift can be transformative. Sometimes a gift is thrust upon us, we have to take it, and we may not immediately appreciate that this is a gift. Accepting the reality, the gifts, the challenges that Hashem sends us, often brings about growth and perspective that cannot be attained when we give a gift of our own volition.

> SOMETIMES A GIFT IS THRUST UPON US, WE HAVE TO TAKE IT, AND WE MAY NOT IMMEDIATELY APPRECIATE THAT THIS IS A GIFT.

## AN INTERESTING CHOICE OF WORD

Why does the Torah use the word *"terumah"* for gift? Why not the word *"tzedakah,"* charity, or *"matanah,"* a present?

*"Terumah"* is meant to evoke the tithing process of giving priestly gifts. Produce is referred to as *tevel* at this pre-tithing stage, until it is given to the *kohanim*, the priests. The status of *tevel* prevents benefit to the owner of the field.[89] The act of tithing, however, is transformative: when the *kohen* is given his portion, the entire field becomes permissible to the owner.

Similarly, this gift—a *terumah* to G-d's Sanctuary—is transformative. When we give of ourselves in the direction of sanctity, connecting to a higher spiritual realm, we are elevated and our relationship with the Divine is reshaped.

During the years I was mentored by Rabbi Binyomin Yudin, he would at times call me the very last minute to fill in and give a *shiur* or to take his

---

88    *Terumah* 25:1.
89    *Sanhedrin* 83a.

place at a life-cycle event. He would often conclude his request by reminding me that ultimately the teacher or the one "giving over" is the person in any exchange who gains the most from the transaction. Through the challenge of preparation and mastery of the material to teach, or the effort invested in being present for someone in their time of need, it is the instructor or mentor who often walks away most satisfied. Our rabbis instruct: "L'fum tzaara agra—Commensurate with the investment and toil is the ultimate reward."[90]

## ACCLIMATION AND DISAPPOINTMENT

It takes time to acclimate to Holland. There's a different pace, a different culture, different gifts. Guardians of a special gift, a transformative gift, have a responsibility to educate others, and the burden to advocate on behalf of those who are less able to take care of and advocate for themselves.

THERE IS PAIN AND DISAPPOINTMENT IN THAT PROCESS.

There is pain and disappointment in that process. My wife and I were terribly dismayed when not one, but two Orthodox day schools in our community refused to accept our son into their pre-school programs. At this juncture of his development, it was hard not to feel like a bias or stigma was at play rather than an academic issue or challenge. We came to realize that there was much education and tolerance that needed to be advocated and disseminated.

We live in a liberal secular society that screams for tolerance in all realms, including the realm of personal lifestyle. Tolerance—openness, respect and sensitivity for others who are not quite like you—is indeed basic even to Torah thought.[91] Yet there seems to

WHO KNOWS? MAYBE OUR SPECIAL CHILDREN MIGHT EVEN TEACH OUR TYPICALLY DEVELOPING CHILDREN AND COMMUNITIES A THING OR TWO ABOUT CHARACTER REFINEMENT OR WORK ETHIC.

---

90    *Avos* 2:6.

91    *Avos* 1:2 speaks of the three pillars upon which the world stands including acts of kindness to those who are in need of support and strengthening.

be a lack of that same tolerance for children that G-d has created with an extra chromosome. Are they any less deserving of the finest Jewish education? Of acceptance in a shul?

Furthermore, who knows? Maybe our special children might even teach our typically developing children and communities a thing or two about character refinement or work ethic.

I'm not sure that we would have *l'chatchila* chosen this *terumah*. But that is exactly the point.

*V'yikchu Li terumah* demands surrender to a higher will, to G-d in His infinite wisdom, much smarter than we are. A G-d who knew exactly what transformative gift our fledgling family needed to grapple with, struggle with and ultimately thrive with. Yedidya has a *neshamah*, a soul, that soars. Many who interact with him are touched by his charm, spirituality and mischievousness. Of course, I'm in touch with reality: Yedidya has flaws just like the rest of us. However, he also has strengths—just like the rest of us.

**YEDIDYA HAS FLAWS JUST LIKE THE REST OF US.**

I now would like to share Part Two of Emily Perl Kingsley's writing:

> I have been in Holland for over a decade now. It has become home. I have had time to catch my breath, to settle and adjust, to accept something different than I'd planned.
>
> I reflect back on those years past when I had first landed in Holland. I remember clearly my shock, my fear, my anger—the pain and uncertainty. In those first few years, I tried to get back to Italy as planned, but Holland was where I was to stay. Today, I can say how far I have come on this unexpected journey. I have learned so much more. But, this too has been a journey of time.
>
> I worked hard. I bought new guidebooks. I learned a new language and I slowly found my way around this new land. I have met others whose plans had changed like mine, and who could share my experience. We supported one another and some have become very special friends. Some of these fellow

travelers had been in Holland longer than I and were seasoned guides, assisting me along the way. Many have encouraged me. Many have taught me to open my eyes to the wonder and gifts to behold in this new land. I have discovered a community of caring. Holland wasn't so bad.

I think that Holland is used to wayward travelers like me and grew to become a land of hospitality, reaching out to welcome, to assist and to support newcomers like me in this new land. Over the years, I've wondered what life would have been like if I'd landed in Italy as planned. Would life have been easier? Would it have been as rewarding? Would I have learned some of the important lessons I hold today?

Sure, this journey has been more challenging and at times I would (and still do) stomp my feet and cry out in frustration and protest. And, yes, Holland is slower paced than Italy and less flashy than Italy, but this too has been an unexpected gift. I have learned to slow down in ways too and look closer at things, with a new appreciation for the remarkable beauty of Holland with its tulips, windmills and Rembrandts.

I have come to love Holland and call it home. I have become a world traveler and discovered that it doesn't matter where you land. What's more important is what you make of your journey and how you see and enjoy the very special, the very lovely, things that Holland, or any land, has to offer. Yes, over a decade ago I landed in a place I hadn't planned. Yet I am thankful, for this destination has been richer than I could have imagined!

Why not visit Holland? You never know what gifts or even life-altering perspectives you may find there.

# MY SUPER SON

love to watch the Super Bowl with an exceptionally big football fan. His name is Yedidya and he is my oldest child. As mentioned earlier, he was born with Down syndrome. He loves football so much that he sleeps in his Dallas Cowboys uniform. (Confession: I helped him pick my favorite team.) Unfortunately, he is constantly tackling his brothers and sister. It got bad enough that we had to teach him the mantra "No tackling."

I enjoy streaming a game on my computer while Yedidya sits on my lap and always roots for the "red team." Sometimes, we are lucky enough to actually have a team with a red uniform playing on the screen before us. Sometimes not, but that doesn't dull his enthusiasm for the game.

Football is a raw sport and it can stir genuine emotions. A few years back, in the wildcard round of the playoffs, Robert Griffin III (RG3), the Redskins star rookie quarterback, also wearing a red uniform, went down with a terrible knee

YEDIDYA ISN'T THE MOST ARTICULATE CHILD, BUT HIS PURITY OF SPIRIT AND SENSITIVITY PUTS HIM SPOT-ON WHEN IT COMES TO FEELING THE PAIN OF OTHERS.

injury. Yedidya immediately pointed to the screen and poignantly ex-claimed "Daddy, sick!" He was genuinely pained by the spectacle of the player sprawled on the ground in obvious agony. Yedidya isn't the most articulate child, but his purity of spirit and sensitivity puts him spot-on when it comes to feeling the pain of others. Watching RG3 crumpled on the ground, his very articulate father could not have ex-pressed the moment any more succinctly, meaningfully or compas-sionately.

One Shabbos, as I was humming a *niggun*, a melody, during the meal, I cut my finger on my drinking glass. The adults at the table realized that it was a surface wound and thankfully no glass had penetrated the finger. Yedidya ran to the phone, picked it up and began saying "ambulance" into the phone. He doesn't know how to call 911 (and of course I strongly prefer that he doesn't pick up the phone unnecessarily on Shabbos), but the sentiment was incredibly touching.

I recently finished reading a life-altering book entitled *Daring Great-ly* by Brene Brown.[92] It discusses having the courage to be vulnerable and how this perceived weakness could actually transform our lives. Many people struggle with vulnerability and public perception. We are often so focused on "other esteem" at the great expense of our own self-esteem.[93]

At one point in the book, she quotes Pema Chodron, who writes:

> Compassion is not a relationship between the healer and the wounded. It's a relationship between equals. Only when we

---

92    *Daring Greatly: How the Courage to Be Vulnerable Transforms the Way We Live, Love, Parent and Lead* (Gotham Books, 2012). The first page explains that the title emanates from Theodore Roosevelt's speech, "Citizenship in a Republic." The speech, sometimes referred to as "The Man in the Arena," was delivered at the Sorbonne in Paris, France on April 23, 1910.

93    I recently had a young congregant tell me that it is essential that I speak more often to the congregation about vulnerability and not caring so much about what everybody else says or thinks. It is clear that people really struggle with these issues and yearn for a safe space to discuss them. When I addressed it from the pulpit, many of the young professionals in my shul responded positively and thanked me afterwards.

know our own darkness well can we be present with the darkness of others. Compassion becomes real when we recognize our shared humanity.[94]

I thought of Yedidya when I read these lines. Maybe subconsciously, because he is "wounded" or "imperfect," he is able to express real compassion and be a healer, of sorts. It's ironic, because many don't perceive a developmentally disabled person as their equal.

Developmentally challenged individuals sometimes lack the inhibition or cognition to hide their vulnerability, but that is what makes them our "equals" in critical moments. Imagine spontaneously expressing intense care or feelings for another while being completely indifferent to how it will be perceived by those observing. Life would be so different. Worse, but better.

> IMAGINE SPONTANEOUSLY EXPRESSING INTENSE CARE OR FEELINGS FOR ANOTHER WHILE BEING COMPLETELY INDIFFERENT TO HOW IT WILL BE PERCEIVED BY THOSE OBSERVING.

The more esoteric sections of Jewish tradition confirm this analysis.[95] They teach that the disabled possess a higher or more pure soul than others. They are not constrained as their physical or intellectual blemishes remove a barrier to their spiritual charisma, which is not the case in typically functioning people. The great scholar Rabbi Avrohom Yeshaya Karelitz, popularly known by the name Chazon Ish, would regularly stand up for such individuals.

What inspires me every day is the attitude of people like my Yedidya. They live life without fear and they confront new challenges each and every day—with a positive attitude. As we shift our attitudes toward the

---

94    P. 234.

95    Many years ago, I saw a pamphlet published by Rabbi Yehuda Serevnick of Har Nof entitled "What Does the Soul Say?" (*Mah Ha-neshamah Omeret?*) In the introduction, he posits that the perfected body is a barrier to communication with the higher realms of existence. He used facilitated communication with various special-needs populations and quizzed them about the higher worlds and recorded their various answers. This is a controversial technique and not accepted by everybody.

special-needs population, our task may just be to emulate these exceptional people in our midst.

Many of us fail to fully be there for others because we are too busy focusing on ourselves. We let the vicissitudes of life too easily knock us down. My son's disability allows him to give others the gift of compassion and shared humanity. I love watching football with Yedidya because he not only makes me laugh with his enthusiasm and descriptions of the game, but also because he teaches me profound lessons about the game of life.

# THIS CAT HAS
# NINE LIVES

**M**y son literally has nine lives.

After sprinting down the block, he stopped at the corner. Usually, he waits there until we catch up with him. For some reason, this time he dashed across the street. I couldn't believe my eyes. I kept screaming his name, but he just kept on going. My mind flashed back to other such incidents: the Shavuos when he climbed out an open window onto our fire escape; the time he disappeared in Riverside Park and we had to call the police; the myriad times he ran out of our shul and down the block; or the week before the street-corner incident, when he was hanging down from a twenty-foot ledge.

You are probably thinking, *negligent parents*.

I wouldn't claim that we are perfect parents, but we are far from negligent. We invest plenty of time and energy and resources in our son.

Our challenge is teaching a young energetic boy with Down syndrome safety awareness.

This last occurrence with our son came upon the heels of the yearly Yachad family *shabbaton*. Yachad, a division of the Orthodox Union, sponsors a weekend geared toward families with special-needs children. Nearly 1,000 people come together to offer and receive *chizuk* from each other and from various experts in the field of disabilities. We have gone numerous times, and each time we come away reinvigorated and feeling supported.

## OUTSIDERS TO THE CLUB

Interestingly, some individuals without special-needs family members participated in the weekend as well. Some were senior leadership members of the Orthodox Union, others were sponsors of the *shabbaton*. Each professed to being deeply inspired and moved by the experience.

I know they were genuinely touched, but when listening to their comments and feedback, something didn't resonate with me. Our rabbis teach that it is difficult to glean insight into another until you've been in their shoes.[96] I know that these individuals mean extraordinarily well, but realistically, an outside observer cannot fully grasp the meaning of such a weekend to those families being serviced and supported. There is so much more to it than meets the eye.

AN OUTSIDE OBSERVER CANNOT FULLY GRASP THE MEANING OF SUCH A WEEKEND TO THOSE FAMILIES BEING SERVICED AND SUPPORTED.

## BONDING

On Friday night, our family sat with a couple that was new to the *shabbaton*. I always find it awkward to ask what disability their child possesses. Everybody has a different story and some are more comfortable

---

96    *Avos* 2:5.

sharing theirs than others. Eventually, after asking some general questions, I was able to create a comfort level and then inquire as to their child's disability. By the end of the meal, we were kindred spirits. The very same thing happened at Shabbos lunch with a different couple. There is something very powerful about uniting with others in a similar situation. Spending time with other couples who have children with special needs normalizes and validates our reality.[97]

## A MEANINGFUL CONTRIBUTOR

After dinner Friday night, I participated in a panel discussion that addressed the question of where we glean our support from and how our children are included in the community. I shared with the audience the active role that our son plays both in my shul as well as at our Shabbos table. In particular, I shared how he is given a chance to sing or share some of his learning with others at the meal. I also communicated how those around the table are inevitably amazed at what our little boy is capable of. After the panel, many families approached to share their own stories. The word Yachad means "together." And that's truly what this weekend was about: the opportunity to be embraced by others who really understand the rewards, but also the trials and tribulations, of parenting a special-needs child.

> THOSE AROUND THE TABLE ARE INEVITABLY AMAZED AT WHAT OUR LITTLE BOY IS CAPABLE OF.

## UNDERSTANDING AND NOT UNDERSTANDING

In my rabbinical work, people often come to me for support or advice. It could be an infertility issue, the loss of a job, difficulty getting married, *shalom bayis* issues or an illness in the family. I try as much as I

---

97    This is true in many different realms. I recently attended a program run by One Family Fund, an organization that helps those who have been victims of terror. As I watched the video about support the organization provides, I was overcome with the understanding that the primary benefit is being with similarly situated people, thus "normalizing" the reality of those who are suffering and often feel so alone and misunderstood.

can to connect with their pain, and occasionally, I even think that I am a pretty effective counselor. Still, sometimes I am unable to relate to their experience. I'm left to imagine what my life would be like if I had that challenge.[98]

This Yachad weekend reminded me of the realistic gap that exists between human beings. And it highlighted the pleasure of occasionally being with others that have a profound understanding of your own experience.

THIS YACHAD WEEKEND REMINDED ME OF THE REALISTIC GAP THAT EXISTS BETWEEN HUMAN BEINGS.

This concept was further reinforced by the following anecdote.

> Recently, a Shabbos guest asked for my input on paying a shivah call to a girl he recently broke up with. He shared that one rabbi he asked advised against it, while a second rabbi encouraged the call. Considering the awkwardness of the situation, the No position was understandable. When I asked him to elaborate on the underlying reasoning of the other rabbinic position, he explained that the second rabbi had once sat shivah for a parent and was confident that at such a vulnerable moment, the girl would likely appreciate the visit from someone who was recently an integral presence in her life.

In moments of great sadness or pain, we crave connection and understanding of our plight. Although a person may not be the long-term solution or may be an ill-suited life partner, he may be a comfort for the present challenge due to their recent closeness. Admittedly, he may also be a painful reminder of loss and the last person the challenged person wants to see.

---

98    When I trained as a therapist, I was exposed to a wonderful concept. The instructor noted that he once had back-to-back clients. The initial one suffered terminal illness and had six months to live and yet was in good spirits. The second one had made $500,000 the previous year but was inconsolable as his younger brother had brought in a cool million dollars. The instructor shared that viscerally, he wanted to yell at the second client and provide some perspective through the experience and reaction of the initial client. He then shifted gears and explained that this is ultimately the challenge of the good therapist. To be present with each client in their situation and to connect with their unique pain without passing judgment as to the validity of that pain.

## JUGGLING SPECIAL LIVES

There is a common misperception about many families with special-needs children: many people assume that we are managing better than we actually are. Some of us, at least to the outside observer, are able to juggle and balance the various complexities of our lives. Still, the intensive therapy schedules, diaper changes, fighting for government services—among other tedious roles—are often missed by outside observers. Maybe some of us are a little too proficient, so that even people close to us aren't fully cognizant of our challenges. But that doesn't minimize just how challenging it is.

> MAYBE SOME OF US ARE A LITTLE TOO PROFICIENT, SO THAT EVEN PEOPLE CLOSE TO US AREN'T FULLY COGNIZANT OF OUR CHALLENGES.

Reach out to the families of special-needs kids. Offer to lend a hand; it will be much appreciated. Don't be afraid to gently broach our challenge. Sometimes it is more painful to have people close to us just ignore what is to many the "elephant in the room."[99]

## LEARNING TO ACCEPT SPECIAL LIVES

My wife and I have the merit to educate and inspire others as to the beauty and genuine contributions that can be made by individuals with special needs. The perspectives of many of my congregants have shifted due to the presence and participation of my son in their shul. One

---

99  We once hosted a family from our shul for Shabbos early in my rabbinic tenure. At dessert, the mother of the family referred to our son with special needs as the "elephant in the room." We were a bit put off but also came to understand that many people are uncomfortable around people with disabilities and lack the sensitivity, tact or even words to be helpful and contribute meaningfully to a challenging situation. We have become advocates to help normalize for others this growing demographic in our communities. I will add that it is a rarity that a friend will inquire about Yedidya. I assume they think I will be offended or uncomfortable. He has challenges and it would seem appropriate to me to inquire as to how he is doing. On the rare occasion that somebody asks, I'm appreciative. I don't enjoy when it is used to highlight a vulnerability that I have or to level an imaginary playing field when the other person feels inferior or uncomfortable about something less than desirable that they possess in their life.

congregant shared that when his granddaughter was born with Down syndrome, he was comforted, because he had observed my son in shul during the year leading up to her birth.

Yet, every once in a while, parents of these special children, need some *chizuk* and renewed perspective. A place where we can share the challenges of parenting a rambunctious and mischievous little boy who has nine lives. Thank you to Yachad for providing us and so many others a forum to connect with similarly situated families who most authentically understand and feel what we do.

# SUMMER CAMP REVISITED

remember vividly my summer experience after my post high school year in Israel. I was encouraged by my older *chavrusa* in yeshiva to be a counselor in Camp HASC, a camp for special-needs children.[100] He had met his wife there and they both assured me it would be a phenomenal experience and a wonderful place to continue my spiritual growth until I returned to yeshiva.

I remember many things about the experience, but what stands out was the mantra we often heard, that of giving a break to the parents and the siblings of the child. This was constantly reinforced to the counselors

WHAT STANDS OUT WAS THE MANTRA WE OFTEN HEARD, THAT OF GIVING A BREAK TO THE PARENTS AND THE SIBLINGS OF THE CHILD. I WOULD NEVER HAVE IMAGINED THAT I WOULD ONE DAY BE THE PARENT OF JUST SUCH A CHILD, ALSO IN NEED OF JUST SUCH RESPITE AND SUPPORT.

---

100    Rabbi Ari Waxman, current Director of the American program at Sha'alvim, mentioned earlier in "My Rebbi's Rebbi."

as part of the significant contribution we were making. It sounded reasonable enough, but honestly, it was difficult from the vantage point of a twenty-year-old to fully comprehend what it meant.

I would never have imagined that I would one day be the parent of just such a child, also in need of just such respite and support.

## SLEEPAWAY ANXIETY

The initial time any child attends sleepaway camp can be daunting, not just for the child but also for the parents. Sometimes children come home early, as they are homesick. Other times, the parents allow only one month at camp because they desperately miss their child. I'm quite familiar with both scenarios just from families in my congregation.

On the other hand, sleepaway camp is a marvelous context in which to make new friends, explore new vistas and to cultivate individuation and independence. This reality is true both for parents and children. Parents often celebrate their newfound freedom, allowing them to rediscover their marriages, friendships and hobbies. It also facilitates greater attention for the children still at home. Children often thrive in a camp setting without the usual parental constraints.

PARENTS OFTEN CELEBRATE THEIR NEWFOUND FREEDOM, ALLOWING THEM TO REDISCOVER THEIR MARRIAGES, FRIENDSHIPS AND HOBBIES.

## FOR THE VERY FIRST TIME

Recently, we sent a child away to sleepaway camp for the first time. He had just turned nine years old and we felt he and we were ready. Still, we were exceptionally nervous. This was because our Yedidya isn't the typical child going away from home. Since Yedidya has Down syndrome, we couldn't be completely sure to what extent he understood that he would get to come home only after a few weeks' time.

WE COULDN'T BE COMPLETELY SURE TO WHAT EXTENT HE UNDERSTOOD THAT HE WOULD GET TO COME HOME ONLY AFTER A FEW WEEKS' TIME.

pletely sure to what extent he understood that he would get to come home only after a few weeks' time. Despite our trepidation, it turned out to be a wonderful, transformative and confidence-building experience for him—and us.

The last few summers, we had been discussing sending Yedidya away to camp. Honestly, we just couldn't part with him. We explored options, but nothing made sense. Thankfully, with the guidance and help of Yachad, we found an ideal camp setting.

## INTEGRATION–NESHER IT IS

Camp Nesher is a camp in Pennsylvania that integrates special-needs children within a predominantly typical camp population in a sleepaway camp setting and context. As Yedidya attends a special-needs oriented secular program during the year, we were excited for this level of integration and the opportunity for him to be in a religious environment.

It was most helpful that Yedidya began attending various Yachad junior *shabbatonim* (or as he calls it, a "*shabbos-a-tone*") throughout the past year. Granted, he was only away from home for less than thirty-six hours at a time, but it enabled him to acclimate to being in different places with different people and also understanding that he gets to return home at the end of the experience.

Yedidya is a major personality and a major part of our family. Each of his three siblings tends to jokingly (or maybe not so jokingly) select Yedidya as their favorite sibling. They all claim he is the most amicable, flexible and giving. When he is away from home, there is something amiss, something tangible missing. Yet, there is also more space for the other children to shine and glean parental attention and focus.

EACH OF HIS THREE SIBLINGS TENDS TO JOKINGLY (OR MAYBE NOT SO JOKINGLY) SELECT YEDIDYA AS THEIR FAVORITE SIBLING.

The day we sent him off was an uncomfortable one. The buses left from Teaneck, New Jersey, so we drove him a short trip over the George Washington Bridge from our Upper West Side home to the bus location. We greeted the counselors and other families and made small talk. Finally, we escorted Yedidya onto the bus.

I noticed my wife was crying which made me struggle to hold back my tears as well. This was a growth milestone that we had anticipated and hoped for. Still, the bond and connection of parents with their special-needs child is extremely intense. Would he get the level of care that he is accustomed to at home?

## WAITING FOR A GOOD WORD

We anxiously anticipated any news from camp and eagerly anticipated the one phone call a week allowed on Friday (funny, because it wasn't a prison camp). Finally they arrived, beautiful pictures of Yedidya doing all types of cool and exciting things. Fortunately, in the technologically sophisticated world in which we live, his counselors could almost instantaneously send us updates. Our son was rock climbing, swimming, playing basketball and, most significantly, smiling and being loved.

OUR SON WAS ROCK CLIMBING, SWIMMING, PLAYING BASKETBALL AND, MOST SIGNIFICANTLY, SMILING AND BEING LOVED.

## SHOE IS ON THE OTHER FOOT

As a parent, wearing the other shoe, I finally understood differently what I, as a counselor, had provided for those parents over twenty years ago. The "break" is only valuable when the parents feel their child is in good hands, loved and appreciated. Thankfully, our child received that very same experience that I myself provided so many years back.

It was of great comfort for us to learn and discern that Yedidya had achieved "rock-star" status in camp. It was even better on Fridays when we called camp, heard his excited voice and he couldn't stop talking about all the fun things he was doing. It wasn't easy for him to answer all our various queries, but we did sense that things were solid and good.

YEDIDYA HAD ACHIEVED "ROCK-STAR" STATUS IN CAMP.

Any parent of a typical child could essentially feel and relate to the experience I just described. Most parents have a confluence of emotions about sending children away from home. Whether to camp, high school, a year or two in Israel or to the wedding canopy, our experiences aren't that different or anomalous—or maybe they are?

They are and they aren't. Parenting a special-needs child is like regular parenting, plus. There are a range of disabilities out there and a range of amounts that people invest in their children in general. A parent of a special-needs child generally can't go on cruise control mode or let up even for a moment; it just won't work.

> A PARENT OF A SPECIAL-NEEDS CHILD GENERALLY CAN'T GO ON CRUISE CONTROL MODE OR LET UP EVEN FOR A MOMENT; IT JUST WON'T WORK.

My wife often says that a special-needs child is the equivalent of two children, almost as if we have five children instead of four. She tells me many of her special-needs mom online forums argue the same.

> MY WIFE OFTEN SAYS THAT A SPECIAL-NEEDS CHILD IS THE EQUIVALENT OF TWO CHILDREN, ALMOST AS IF WE HAVE FIVE CHILDREN INSTEAD OF FOUR.

## MY FOREVER CHILD

For me the issue isn't so quantitative as much as it is qualitative. Each Shabbos I give my children a *brachah* at the Friday night meal before *Kiddush*. Once a year, I recite the special elongated *brachah* found in the High Holiday *machzor* for Erev Yom Kippur,[101] skeptical that my Yedidya will marry and produce *zera kodesh*, his own holy children. I'm often skeptical about his making a *parnassah* or livelihood as well. These children are our "forever children." It is a painful reality and realization for those of us chosen for this role.

However, it also adds to the joy when he reaches a "typical" milestone and succeeds at it. It is a real source of pride when he has an experience not that different than my other children might have one day. So the

---

101    To be found in the beginning of almost all *machzorim* for Yom Kippur, it is a poetic and long "*Yehi ratzon*" blessing that requests many spiritual and physical aspirations that we would like for our children. My own father, who is often in Israel for Yom Kippur calls me and gives me this blessing over the phone each year. I often get very emotional when transmitting the *brachah* to my own children.

feelings aren't that different from a typical parent, yet (concurrently) they are very different indeed.

## THE TIDE AND TIMES ARE CHANGING

I'm thankful for having been on both sides of the experience and ultimately being the beneficiary of the kindness of the dynamic and dedicated young men and women who ensured my family and my special-needs son a terrific summer. However, I'm even more appreciative that my son had this experience, specifically in an inclusive environment with typical children. I served many summers ago in a camp that was exclusively for special-needs kids. Thankfully, over many years, our community and society have evolved and the more inclusive model, such as Camp Nesher and others, is becoming more of the norm. Thankfully, barriers are being broken and new bars are constantly being set. If we aim high, we will go far. I can feel the tide changing in Yedidya's favor. Maybe with further medical breakthroughs and societal progress, he could even merit a beautiful wife and maybe even some *zera kodesh*. Who would have ever thought it possible?

IF WE AIM HIGH, WE WILL GO FAR.

# SECTION FOUR

## The Shidduch Crisis and the

## Early Years of Marriage

# FROM THE DEPTHS
# I CRY OUT TO YOU

I wasn't sure if I should make my annual Rosh Hashanah/Yom Kippur trip to Israel. When the *Yamim Noraim* would come around, I would usually take off from my job to rejoin (for a while, at least) my yeshiva. But that year was different.

It was the tenth anniversary of my dating career. At the age of twenty, I had gone on my first date. I can recall how excited I had been and how confident I was that she would be "the one."

Unfortunately, what followed were ten challenging years of dashed expectations, disappointments and, sometimes, heartbreak. While I was doing okay in other significant realms, my spirit was broken: My dating life had been less than satisfactory, and it hurt. I was skeptical if I had the inner fortitude to spend another holiday season in Israel with my married friend and his children.

> MY SPIRIT WAS BROKEN:
> MY DATING LIFE HAD BEEN
> LESS THAN SATISFACTORY.

## HERE WE GO AGAIN

Somehow, I found the courage to get on the plane. Davening was difficult that year. I was beaten down by my dating experiences and didn't have the will to beseech Hashem. I wondered to myself, *Would the coming year be different than previous years?*

The long davening of Rosh Hashanah and the jet lag teamed up to wipe me out. I needed a break, and so I left the yeshiva the next morning and checked into a Jerusalem hotel. It was Tzom Gedalia and as soon as I checked in, I went to bed. I awoke at two p.m. and decided to daven *Minchah* at the Kotel.

After davening *Minchah*, I spent time reciting *Tehillim*, asking Hashem to help me find my wife.

## ELIYAHU HANAVI?

I left the Kotel area and waited for a taxi. When it arrived, I noticed that the driver's lips were moving. I asked the driver what he was saying. He answered that he was reciting *Tehillim*. *A good sign*, I thought to myself.

I clearly didn't look like a happy camper and as we headed toward my hotel, he asked me why I looked so sad. I explained that I had been in *shidduchim* for a long time, unsuccessfully, and had just been davening by the Kotel.

My driver Yaakov understood my pain. He shared that he married at the age of thirty-four and experienced the intense longing to be "normal," to have a home, a wife and children.

Then he surprised me. He said, "Come with me to Amuka now." I was suspect of this grandiose and impractical plan of action and responded negatively, finding all kinds of excuses. It was around five-thirty by now and I was tired and hungry. I told him that I was a *kohen* and could not go to Amuka, which is a burial place. Amuka was also a three hour ride from Jerusalem. And the trip would simply cost too much.

Yaakov wouldn't be deterred. He offered me a discounted rate and wouldn't take no for an answer. He told me to be spontaneous and not to think too much. When G-d sends an opportunity, grab it, he said.

WHEN G-D SENDS AN OPPORTUNITY, GRAB IT, HE SAID!

Ironically, in all my years of dating, I had never journeyed to Amuka. Amuka is the burial site of the holy Tanna Rabbi Yonasan ben Uziel, who never married. There is a tradition that Rabbi Yonasan ben Uziel will intercede on behalf of anyone who travels to his burial site seeking a spouse.[102] Indeed, even for the rationally minded among us, there are countless stories of people returning from Amuka and meeting their spouse soon after. It is a favorite spot to visit by seminary girls!

## THE RATIONALIST INSIDE

I had every reason in the world *not* to take him up on his idea. In retrospect, however, that was the critical point for the shift in my *mazel*. I have a friend who says that when you're doing a lot of *hishtadlus* and nothing is working, you should take a break, and maybe do something counterintuitive. Whether that advice is correct or not, it does seem to have worked for me. The renowned brilliant physicist, Albert Einstein, similarly commented, "Doing the same thing over and over again and expecting different results is called insanity."[103] For some reason, going against my nature, I allowed myself to be persuaded by a complete stranger. While I am far from the spontaneous type, I decided to go for it. I shut my brain off and took a chance on something new and different.

DOING THE SAME THING OVER AND OVER AGAIN AND EXPECTING DIFFERENT RESULTS IS CALLED INSANITY.

---

102    While our rabbis tell us that davening at *kivrei tzaddikim* is a *segulah* for all types of help, the tradition of Amuka as an address for unmarried men and women is a relatively new one, according to experts in the field. It was "rediscovered" in 1951 by Rabbi Shalom Gefner of Meah Shearim, among many other holy gravesites, which he ferreted out according to the writings of Rabbi Chaim Vital, based on the teachings of the Arizal.

103    This quote has been attributed to various famous people including Benjamin Franklin.

## SOME SOUND SPIRITUAL ADVICE

Yaakov and I talked for the entire trip. He shared that he had been a *ba'al teshuvah* earlier in his life, but had now lost some of his fervor. He could have fooled me. I had never met anyone with stronger faith. During our entire ride, he prepared me for our arrival at the holy site. He told me to yell out to Hashem, to be stubborn and demand that He help me find a wife. Yaakov also suggested giving charity in the merit of the Tanna and committing to additional acts of service to Hashem. He implored me not to tell anyone of our trip, and not to share with anyone the nature of the things that I accepted upon myself. "*Brachah* only resides upon things that are hidden,"[104] he said. I was uplifted by Yaakov's spirit and faith.

> BRACHAH ONLY RESIDES UPON THINGS THAT ARE HIDDEN.

## ANTICIPATION

As we approached Amuka, I was nervous and scared. It had been a long trip and my anticipated brief foray with Hashem was rapidly approaching. I hoped that I would be up to the task. Amuka was pitch black upon arrival at eleven p.m., and the only people there were five yeshiva students.

Yaakov entered the area of the grave to give charity on my behalf and to daven for me. Being a *kohen*, I stood off to the side and began to daven softly.

I began davening for my single friends. I sincerely wanted each of them to find their wives. I had been caught up in the malaise of my own singlehood for so long that I hadn't davened for my single friends in a long time. Now, at this most critical and weighty juncture I genuinely felt that I wouldn't begrudge them if Hashem answered them before me.

> I WOULDN'T BEGRUDGE THEM IF HASHEM ANSWERED THEM BEFORE ME.

Then I began to ask Hashem to help me. From the depths of my heart,

---

104    *Taanis* 8b.

I openly and honestly began to explain my pain and my innermost desire to have a wife and a family.

I also asked Hashem to help me find a way to leave my job as a lawyer in America and find my way back to learning in Israel. Although I had been fortunate to gain employment at two of Manhattan's most prestigious law firms,[105] I was confident that I hadn't yet discovered my life calling.

I then accepted upon myself two things. I would give $1,000 to help a couple marry, and I would begin to give a *shiur* when I returned to America. I had no idea how I would fulfill either of these commitments, but they resonated within me. I began to cry to Hashem with an intensity that I had never before experienced.

## AN AMAZING SONG

As I disengaged from my prayer, something amazing transpired. The yeshiva boys began to dance. They sang *Od Yishama*,[106] a song commonly heard at weddings. I was drawn into the circle and began to dance and sing along with them. I knew something special was happening, and I dreamed that maybe I would merit to dance at my own wedding with my own friends and family in the upcoming year.

On the ride back, Yaakov and I began to unwind and sing together. He told me that he sensed something miraculous as he watched the American boys dancing together and that he "knew" that everything would be different now. He felt that something had "opened up within me" and that nothing would ever be the same. We arrived at my hotel at two a.m., Yaakov and I exchanged phone numbers and he promised to call me later in the week.

## MATCHMAKER, MATCHMAKER, MAKE ME A MATCH

The next evening, I went to visit a married friend. I knew that his wife

---

105   Simpson Thacher & Bartlett and Fried, Frank, Harris, Shriver and Jacobson.
106   *Yirmiyahu* 33:10–11.

dabbled in *shidduchim* and would probably attempt to set me up. I decided that since I would only be in Israel for six more days, I would turn her down—I wanted to spend my remaining time in Israel recharging my spiritual batteries. For me, the magic of Amuka would need to work in America.

> FOR ME, THE MAGIC OF AMUKA WOULD NEED TO WORK IN AMERICA.

As I expected, when I arrived, his wife immediately suggested a young lady for me. She described a woman from Vienna, Austria and shared with me how impressed she had been when she met her. I was a little intrigued... since I didn't even know where Vienna was! The potential match had spent time in America as well and she assured me that it was a worthwhile idea. She prevailed upon me to give it a try.

The next afternoon, Ruchi and I went on our first date. We talked for three hours. Potential. I then went off to the Kotel to daven. After I finished *Minchah*, my cell phone rang. It was Yaakov the taxi driver. He wanted to know how I was feeling. I was tempted to mention my date, but as he had instructed, I kept things to myself. That evening, I got the go-ahead from my friend's wife to give Ruchi another call. We set up a date the following day and another date after Shabbos.

I was now in a quandary. The first three dates had gone nicely, but Ruchi lived in Jerusalem and I in New York. I had never been a fan of long-distance relationships. I had just turned thirty-one and wasn't sure if it would be prudent for me to put off dating other girls until I would have an opportunity to return to Israel and see Ruchi again.

## DOUBT CREEPS IN

We left things open and I traveled back to my yeshiva for Yom Kippur. Ruchi called on Erev Yom Kippur and explained that she had some time before her semester began and inquired if I'd be interested in her coming to New York after Sukkos. I was a bit nervous about her flying to New York, but something within compelled me to respond with an enthusiastic yes. All through Yom Kippur I was distracted and wasn't sure if I had made the right decision. What if we went out one more time and the entire relationship ended? For that I had told her to fly to New York?

Still, I had said yes, and I did want to see her again. I returned to New York, and our "dating" continued: we talked on the phone for hours each day and sent emails back and forth. I was beginning to become more excited about her impending trip.

Ruchi arrived in New York after Sukkos and we dated intensively that week. As she was getting ready to leave, I (again) was faced with a quandary. Should we continue dating long distance for another five weeks until I could return to Israel for Thanksgiving weekend? Did I want to commit myself now to a trip five weeks later?

## THE "BUSINESS" TRIP

We left things open again. We continued to correspond and we began to grow closer. Initially nervous, I was becoming excited about returning to Israel to see her. Keeping to Yaakov's advice, I told my friends and family that I was going on a business trip. The relationship had potential and I wanted to keep it as quiet as possible.

On the plane to Israel, I discovered that the organization Yad Eliezer made weddings for poor couples in Israel for $1,000. I decided that I would go visit Yad Eliezer and donate the money that I had committed myself to at Amuka. The week in Israel was intense. I met some of Ruchi's siblings. We flew to Vienna together to spend Shabbos with her family. I was so exhausted from the trip and the stress of trying to decide if this was to be my wife that I accidentally slept through davening Shabbos morning. Not great, but to make it worse, Ruchi's father, who is the Chief Rabbi of Austria, had reserved *maftir* for me in the historic main synagogue, Stadttempel.[107] He was quite surprised when I didn't appear in

---

107    The synagogue was constructed in 1824 and 1826. The luxurious Stadttempel was fitted into a block of houses and hidden from plain view of the street, because of an edict issued by Emperor Joseph II that only Roman Catholic places of worship were allowed to be built with facades fronting directly onto public streets. Ironically, this edict saved the synagogue from total destruction during Kristallnacht in November 1938, since the synagogue could not be destroyed without setting on fire the buildings to which it was attached. The Stadttempel

shul. I contemplated telling him that I had davened elsewhere, but I figured honesty was the best policy. I'm not sure that I made the best first impression on him, but I compensated with charm and wit through the rest of the weekend.

## THE COMMITMENT

That Sunday, the day before I was to leave back to New York, Ruchi and I drove to Budapest. It was a beautiful drive and the trip solidified our relationship and concretized our desire to get married. The next step was to work out the technical details and tell our friends and families of our decision.

I returned to New York and went to my daily seven a.m. *minyan* in Queens. As I walked down the street after *minyan*, I met a woman that I hadn't seen in almost a year.[108] I had eaten at her home on a Friday evening and we had discussed the possibility of my giving a women's *shiur* in the neighborhood. She was wondering if I would still be interested. I jumped at the opportunity, amazed at my good fortune.

I was so thankful to Hashem for enabling me to fulfill both commitments that I had made at Amuka, only a short while before.

Ruchi returned to New York for Chanukah and we got engaged. After much thought and deliberation, the wedding was set for three months later in Jerusalem. I decided that I would leave my law firm after the wedding, and move to Israel to learn in *kollel*. I could never have imagined that just a few months after my trip to Amuka, I would merit to get married and study in Israel.

## RECONNECTING WITH YAAKOV THE TAXI DRIVER

I returned to Israel after Chanukah to work on the wedding arrangements and for an engagement party that my in-laws were making for us. I wanted

---

was the only synagogue in the city to survive World War II, as the Nazis destroyed all of the other ninety-three synagogues and Jewish prayer houses in Vienna.

108    Sadly, this wonderful woman subsequently passed away from cancer at a very young age.

to invite Yaakov to the party and inform him of the wonderful news. I left a message for him with all the details. Soon after, my cell phone rang.

It was Yaakov speaking at a frantic pace. He said he was driving in his taxi and had picked up two passengers. He related that he heard them discussing an engagement party and inquired who the young man was. They told him, "Dovid Cohen from New York." Yaakov jubilantly related that he had just picked up Ruchi and her mother in his taxi!

## THE LONG-AWAITED ANSWER

King David says in *Tehillim*: "From the depths I call to You Hashem."[109] Amuka owes its name to the fact that it is located in the depths—near the holy city of Tzefas. That night, after the fast of Gedalia, I cried out to Hashem from the depths of my being, in a place of incredible physical depth, and Hashem sent me my long-awaited salvation.

Our rabbis teach that Hashem's salvation comes "in the blink of an eye."[110] In those few moments, Hashem removed years of frustration and loneliness, removed me from an unfulfilling job, and carried me to a new world of growth, learning and inspiration.

I had searched and davened for ten years. I had tried.

Finally, twenty-four hours after opening my heart at Amuka (my first visit there, ever), I was set up on a date with my *bashert*.[111]

In the end, it was crying out from the depths (and the help of a special Israeli taxi driver) that carried the day.

---

109    *Tehillim* 130:1–4.

110    *Berachos* 10a.

111    Josh White was passing by the Kehillas Bnei Torah shul in Har Nof in November 2014 on his bicycle during an ongoing terrorist attack that claimed the lives of five great and holy rabbis. He ripped the shirt off his back and was ultimately able to contribute to saving the life of Shmuel Goldstein, the son-in-law of renowned educator Tziporah Heller, who had stumbled outside the shul bleeding profusely from his head. Two hours after this incident transpired, Josh White's *shidduch* resume was emailed to his future *kallah*. Josh was in his early thirties and also spent many years dabbling and struggling unsuccessfully in the *parshah* of *shidduchim*. Sometimes, just one amazing act can change years of frustration. We must always keep moving and doing, as we never know which action will tip the scales and rip open the heavens in our favor.

# THE LONG ROAD
# HOME

The Chasam Sofer states that a person who merits a personal salvation should observe a *yom tov* commemorating the experience.[112] He limits this concept, however, to a person who has escaped the throes of death.

Although one could posit that finding a spouse after a protracted search qualifies as escaping from death—it certainly felt that way for me!—I'm hesitant to apply this concept to my personal context, partly because the day that triggered my deliverance was Tzom Gedalia.

Tzom Gedalia was almost the tenth anniversary of my very first *shidduch* date.

After "opening up" to *go to* Amuka, and "opening up" again *at* Amuka, I was set up with my future wife within twenty-four

AFTER "OPENING UP" TO *GO TO* AMUKA, AND "OPENING UP" AGAIN *AT* AMUKA, I WAS SET UP WITH MY FUTURE WIFE WITHIN TWENTY-FOUR HOURS AND ON A DATE WITH HER LESS THAN FORTY-EIGHT HOURS LATER.

---

hours and on a date with her less than forty-eight hours later. Life is full of great ironies.

While I wasn't given the job due to my lengthy—and then miraculous—dating history, I somehow ended up as a rabbi on the Upper West Side of Manhattan, a locale with a significant singles population, and I spend much of my time encouraging and guiding singles of all ages during the often arduous and challenging process of getting married. My duties also include helping married couples navigate the sometimes bumpy waters of the early years of marriage.

I am, *baruch Hashem*, happily married now for over a decade and have a wonderful family; the pain and loneliness of the "search" is no longer. Still, my own history, and my years of helping with other people's experiences, are emblazoned on the forefront of my mind.

Of course, I truly believe in the incredible uniqueness of each person's story, and I don't think there is a one-size-fits-all solution to the "*shidduch* crisis" (although I will grant that there are sometimes overlapping patterns that evolve among certain types of people). Nevertheless, my personal history has yielded a few insights that I use in guiding others and has proven to be helpful.

> I DON'T THINK THERE IS A ONE-SIZE-FITS-ALL SOLUTION TO THE "*SHIDDUCH* CRISIS."

## THE CHANGE-UP

If you are stuck in neutral, try to think out of the box, and be open to unusual suggestions. My own wife is from a country that I barely had heard of before we met. Our *shidduch* made sense in some respects, but was undeniably farfetched. "*Meshaneh makom, meshaneh mazel*"[113] can mean making changes in your headspace or psychological reality to expedite your spiritual success and allow a new *siyata diShmaya* to shine through.

As I reflect on my years of dating, one regret is lost opportunities. Working as a lawyer, I was offered opportunities to move to both Los

---

113    *Rosh Hashanah* 16b.

Angeles and London for extended periods of time. In truth, fear of the unknown was the impetus for turning down the offers. I work with many people who are afraid to change things up a bit. Why not do something different and see where it leads you? Especially if your current approach doesn't seem to be doing the trick.

> WHY NOT DO SOMETHING DIFFERENT AND SEE WHERE IT LEADS YOU?

I also passed up on spending another year studying in Israel. I was concerned how it would impact my dating at that time.[114] "Hindsight is 20/20," but a crucial lesson learned is not to let the dating process control your life. Things will happen in their proper time and a person needs to live and do things that cultivate him or her into a deeper, more prepared partner for marriage.

## HIDDEN LIGHTS

Second, know that there are great people in the world, hidden *tzaddi-kim* like Yaakov (my taxi driver), who want to lift you up and not tear you down. I had my share of critics and detractors during my ten-year *shid-duch* dry period, people who blamed me—directly or indirectly—for my predicament. I don't remember them anymore, but I do fondly recall many others who gave me love and support, people whom I have turned to even in recent years when I needed an extra jolt of *emunah* or *chizuk*. Find those special people who can ease your journey. Sometimes the journey is short, sometimes it is long—but a few special people supporting you can make a huge difference. If you are fortunate enough to have met your *bashert*, try to become a

> YOU CAN MAKE ALL THE DIFFERENCE FOR SOMEONE ELSE!

Yaakov for somebody in need. You can make all the difference for someone else![115]

---

114    I recall going to speak with HaRav Aharon Lichtenstein, the Rosh Yeshiva of Gush Etzion, who very much encouraged me to come back to Eretz Yisrael. Despite his sage advice, dating considerations prevented me from pulling the trigger.

115    One of my favorite stories relating to *shidduchim* is about an older friend who was often badgered by *shadchanim* when turning down dates. He shared with me that Rebbetzin Ella

## HOLD ON TIGHT

Finally, keep in mind that no matter how difficult your (or your child's) *shidduch* process is, it isn't for naught. Every challenge in life brings hidden blessing, such as fresh insights and new perspectives and helps create a deeper more sensitive person. The process is significant and meaningful as a self-development tool, even when sadly or sometimes tragically the intended goal isn't ever reached. I've heard stories of people who were thankful for a cancer diagnosis because it helped them change their perspective on life. Similarly, difficulty and a protracted search can lend incredible perspective that can enhance the rest of one's life. As my dear mother would always encourage me, "*Derech aruchah she-sofo ketzarah*,"[116] the long road home can indeed be the shortest in the end. Because, in truth, none of us know with whom Hashem wants our *neshamah* to interact with in this world.

> EVERY CHALLENGE IN LIFE BRINGS HIDDEN BLESSING.

> AS MY DEAR MOTHER WOULD ALWAYS ENCOURAGE ME, "*DERECH ARUCHAH SHE-SOFO KETZARAH*," THE LONG ROAD HOME CAN INDEED BE THE SHORTEST IN THE END.

## PARTING THOUGHT

Ultimately, *shidduchim* is a difficult time period even if things go smoothly and quickly. Too many people have struggled or even suffered during this process and much ink has been spilled trying to address and solve the feelings of crisis in our community. Having been

> HAVING BEEN THROUGH IT MYSELF, I'M KEENLY AWARE HOW ONE'S SELF-ESTEEM AND SELF-IMAGE CAN TAKE A FEW HITS.

---

Soloveitchik (wife of R' Ahron of Brisk Chicago) would also make various suggestions to him. When he would sometimes say no, she would often respond, "That is your prerogative." This friend was very fond of the *rebbetzin* for being sensitive to his feelings and validating his choices in contrast to others who were often harsh and dismissive. He is happily married today with four children.

116  A similar idea is found in the writings of Wayne Stiles, *Going Places with G-d: A Devotional Journey through the Lands of the Bible* (Ventura, CA: Regal, 2006), pp. 66, 89. My dear mother used to constantly repeat this refrain to me in Hebrew to encourage me in my prolonged personal *shidduch* crisis.

through it myself, I'm keenly aware how one's self-esteem and self-image can take a few hits. My best advice is to stay focused on your goals and loyal to yourself and your needs. If you weather the process and even some storms that will inevitably come your way, you will be much better off for the wear and tear and stronger for the subsequent stages and experiences of life.

# LEAVING THE FREEZER–A TIME TO REFLECT

**T**he story goes that someone suggested a wonderful *shidduch* to a young woman—the proverbial "best boy in Lakewood." The only problem, she was told, was that he was in the "freezer." The young woman replied that she was interested in a warm, caring boy—not one who spends time in a freezer. Only later did she learn that the freezer was figurative, not literal.

Lakewood's system of requiring *bachurim* to spend their first *zman* in yeshiva "cooling off," focusing on learning and preparing for dating, works well. So well, in fact,

DESPITE THE IMMENSE PRESSURE ON YOUNG WOMEN TO BEGIN DATING IMMEDIATELY UPON RETURN FROM SEMINARY, THEY'D ALSO BENEFIT FROM AT LEAST A REFRIGERATOR–IF NOT A FREEZER–EXPERIENCE.

that I think that despite the immense pressure on young women to begin dating immediately upon return from seminary, they'd also benefit from at least a refrigerator—if not a freezer—experience.

I'm not sure if there is a curriculum for the freezer, but I have some areas that I think young men and women should focus on before entering *shidduchim*.

## TIME MANAGEMENT AND CHARACTER REFINEMENT

One area people should focus on is how entering "the *parshah*" will fit into the scheme of daily activities. Dating is a means to an end and not an end unto itself. One should continue cultivating meaningful relationships, pursue growth in Torah and *middos*, and be involved in *chesed* projects. Each of these activities will serve as a solid foundation and base for the future home and leave one feeling spiritually and emotionally nourished.

> DATING IS A MEANS TO AN END AND NOT AN END UNTO ITSELF.

Character refinement and kindness ultimately assures a successful marital union. (Almost) everything else is secondary to these qualities. Many of us are accustomed to focusing on the glitz and glamour promoted prominently by society at large. Before we begin this most important stage of life, we should inculcate within our psyche that Torah values must reign supreme. It is prioritizing these values when we are single that helps us not be taken by the less-important distractors, such as looks, wealth and community stature,[117] which can and often do present themselves while dating.

## DIGGING DEEPER

Ultimately, inner work is at the root of truly giving oneself over and

---

117    *Avos* 4:2. We are implored not to focus on the container but rather to look at what is inside the vessel.

making room for another. Transitioning from "I" to "we" is a brand-new qualitative reality. Rabbi Yosef Dov Solovetichik used this transformative insight in his explanation of the *brachah* recited on *eirusin* (betrothal),[118] categorizing it as a new type of *"birkat ha-mitzvah"* appropriate for a change in status taking place on various planes—emotional, physical, existential and halachic.

> TRANSITIONING FROM "I" TO "WE" IS A BRAND NEW QUALITATIVE REALITY.

In many ways, a marital relationship makes demands of a person similar to the requirements between a person and G-d—humbling ourselves to a Higher will.[119] What flows from this insight is that contemplating one's religious level and outlook can also be a helpful exercise in preparation for marriage. Therapists have long noted the interplay between one's relationship with G-d and with one's parents; these complexities are often transferred onto the marital playing field as well. This is also alluded to in the placement of *kibbud av v'eim* on the *bein adam laMakom* side of the ledger of the Ten Commandments. This placement echoes the parent being a reflection and partner of G-d.[120]

*While visiting Israel, my wife had lunch with an old friend who had not yet married. My wife marveled at how upbeat and accomplished her friend was. Our rabbinical experience in Manhattan has demonstrated that this is an integral component to dealing with the challenge of being an older single. This woman did not allow dating or her single status*

> SHE USED HER ADDITIONAL UNANTICIPATED AND MAYBE EVEN UNWANTED TIME ALONE TO CREATE THE MOST IDEAL VERSION OF HERSELF FOR THE BENEFIT OF HER FUTURE RELATIONSHIP.

---

118   *Mesorah Journal* (OU) vol. II, p. 5.

119   One time, my children asked our son with Down syndrome who is in charge of the world. The answer he was expected to give was Hashem. Instead, he first said Abba and when the kids let on that this was incorrect, he modified his answer and responded authoritatively and confidently that it is Imma. Half-jokingly, I would suggest his perception is that in the home, I often must sublimate my will to a higher one, that of my wife.

120   This is also alluded to by the Chazal (*Niddah* 31) that there are three partners in the creation of every human being and also the idea (I recall hearing in the name of Rabbi Dessler) that our relationship with parents in this world is preparatory for our relationship with the ultimate parent, i.e., Hashem, in the next world. Kabbalistically, the aura of G-d in the next world is expressed as a maternal type of feeling toward our soul.

*to define her, which greatly contributed to her wonderful disposition.*[121]
*Rather, she used her additional unanticipated and maybe even un-*
*wanted time alone to create the most ideal version of herself for the*
*benefit of her future relationship.*

## MY VULNERABLE INNER WORLD

Aside from the attitudinal piece of not being consumed by dating and focusing instead on refining character attributes, there is also a need for *cheshbon hanefesh*, serious introspection, including deep focus on one's emotional makeup.

Vulnerability is not the easiest of traits.[122] True love requires being vulnerable. A person with a strong ego is able to reveal their fears, weaknesses, frailties and great dreams. That is strength, not weakness. People with perfectionist tendencies—masking some kind of inner lack—often have a difficult time sharing their developing emotional world. They may overly intellectualize things in a way that stunts the development of promising relationships. Vulnerability is certainly not highlighted in the culture of Talmudic banter, where one is busy battling to understand the inner workings of the Gemara.

> VULNERABILITY IS CERTAINLY NOT HIGHLIGHTED IN THE CULTURE OF TALMUDIC BANTER, WHERE ONE IS BUSY BATTLING TO UNDERSTAND THE INNER WORKINGS OF THE GEMARA.

---

121    I have found that older singles dislike being referred to as "singles" or "not yet marrieds." They prefer being included in the general community like anybody else without reference to their marital status. They are much more than their status. It is no different than referring to my son Yedidya as "the kid with Down syndrome." That certainly fails to define who he really is at the core of his being.

122    I mentioned earlier in footnote 93 that I had a discussion with a congregant of mine at *Kiddush* about how younger people in particular struggle with vulnerability, or as he expressed it, "putting themselves out there." He shared that many people follow the masses and steer clear of spiritual pursuits out of fear of being perceived as *nebbish* or uncool. He pleaded with me to please address the *kehillah* about this misguided approach and to try and give people the courage to express their inner voice, without so much focus on what people will think. He was correct. When I addressed the topic, many felt "liberated" and were quite appreciative of my words.

Young women often have greater emotional acumen, but less experience "opening up." Yet in order to succeed in finding a marriage partner, people need to make themselves a little vulnerable by expressing their inner yearnings. I know of a number of *rebbeim* in prestigious yeshivas in Israel who invest tremendous time in strengthening the character of each student and helping bolster and secure emotional fragility and underdevelopment. Unfortunately, this is the exception and not the rule.

## DECEPTION?

I shudder when I serve as a reference in a *shidduch* and I realize that the candidate I'm referring is misrepresenting their age.[123] Though I'm told there are *heterim* available for such a practice, I'm left to wonder if such a person is capable of revealing or sharing vulnerability. Even when they insist that they will reveal the truth shortly, I wonder how long it will take to reveal the more difficult inner feelings and hurts that many people carry.

Thankfully, we live in a society where therapy is no longer taboo. It is not uncommon to hear people say in casual conversation that their therapist advised them of something. Many university campuses, including religious institutions have active counseling centers that students and alumni can access. In addition, religious environments have wonderful faculty members sensitive to our religious context. If a student is concerned that he or she isn't fully prepared to enter into a relationship or is having difficulty clarifying their readiness for marriage, he or she should be encouraged to take advantage of these wonderful resources. Life is complicated,

> LIFE IS COMPLICATED, AND THE TRUTH IS, MANY OF US HAVE "ISSUES." JOIN THE CLUB!

---

123    I have been told that various reputable *poskim* have given this dispensation with the understanding that sometimes an opportunity is lost because of a very superficial consideration such as age. However, this presumes that the individual adjusting their age is doing it within a scope that is reasonably close to the real age and plans to reveal the truth within a few dates. Presumably, with the ice broken and a relationship developing, the other party will be more open to the age differential. Though I am understanding and even sympathetic to this tactic, it makes me uncomfortable, particularly when serving as a reference for someone who I know to be doing this.

and the truth is, many of us have "issues." Join the club! Still, a little bit of individual therapy before marriage can help avoid a whole lot of couples' therapy after marriage.

## WHAT DO MY PARENTS THINK?

Another area of focus during the freezer months should be parental input and its role in the process. About twenty years ago, the book *The Art of Loving* by Eric Fromm was a must-read in the dormitories of Ner Yisroel yeshiva in Baltimore for all boys entering the dating world.[124]

> SOMETIMES A PARENT CAN FIGURATIVELY STRANGLE A CHILD AND SOMETIMES A CHILD CAN'T THINK OR OPERATE APART FROM A PARENT.

Fromm focuses on family-of-origin issues and the ability to individuate or to separate comfortably and healthily from our families and build enduring relationships of our own. This struggle for space versus clinging together can be bi-directional. Sometimes a parent can figuratively strangle a child and sometimes a child can't think or operate apart from a parent.

Every dynamic is different, but presumably at younger ages, there will be significant parental involvement. It's important that parents not only love and guide children, but also respect their child's choices. In many cases, the goals of the parents and child aren't unified. Parents can have subconscious agendas (possibly holding onto a child or fulfilling their own needs through the child) that cause friction and frustration in the dating process. Communicating within the family as to who we really are is a necessary skill and ultimately a building block toward strong marital communication.[125] This means having the inner strength to express our truest desires irrespective of resistance that may confront us, especially tension and brushback from a loved one.

---

124    Reported to me by various friends who attended the yeshiva in that time period.

125    I have seen similar issues in the context of kids going off the *derech*. When parents can't or refuse to accept a child for who the child really is, it causes great emotional strain and hurt. I'm in no way belittling the disappointment of having a child go off the *derech*, but the parents' inability to tolerate the child choosing a different life direction often exacerbates the problems and makes it less likely the child will ever return to the religious fold.

*I know a boy who is leaving an excellent yeshiva to attend college. The choice makes much sense for this boy, because he will be more productive in his limited learning hours than he was when he had all day to learn. His parents are distraught, because they feel this transition will severely impact the types of shidduchim that will be suggested to them. Obviously, these parents and their son have very different perspectives on what the ideal shidduch is.*

Awareness and introspection by all involved is necessary in circumventing these considerable psychological hurdles.

## BEING REALLY HONEST

Most significantly, we must learn from Torah luminaries. In reading the marvelous biography of Rebbetzin Batsheva Kanievsky,[126] we should all be inspired by her honesty and normalcy when it came to marriage. She often confided in people who were struggling in marriage that the beginning of her own marriage was also difficult. She had hoped to marry a tall man like her father, Rabbi Elyashiv, and her husband, R' Chaim, was on the shorter side. She also shared with people that her own mother was disappointed and even lonely early in marriage as she had to adjust from the extroversion of her father, Rabbi Aryeh Levine, to the introversion of Rabbi Elyashiv. Things won't always be perfect and we need to be flexible enough to live with our new reality, even if we would have really liked something a bit different. This is also a very significant part of marriage. Nobody gets exactly everything they wanted. What is most necessary is prioritizing and getting the really important things.

THINGS WON'T ALWAYS BE PERFECT AND WE NEED TO BE FLEXIBLE ENOUGH TO LIVE WITH OUR NEW REALITY, EVEN IF WE WOULD HAVE REALLY LIKED SOMETHING A BIT DIFFERENT.

Reflection during the freezer period is critical because marriage is challenging in general, but particularly at the beginning, as we are taught

126    ArtScroll/Mesorah 2012.

by Chazal that "*Kol haschalos kashos*—All beginnings are difficult."[127] The challenges will come and any individual contemplating marriage, man or woman, must ask themselves before embarking on dating if they have the tools and inner fortitude to weather the storms.

In the increasingly more complex world in which we live, this type of preparatory work shouldn't be taken for granted. With the divorce rate what it is and our community far from immune to it, it behooves us to begin taking pre-dating reflection more seriously.

WITH THE DIVORCE RATE WHAT IT IS AND OUR COMMUNITY FAR FROM IMMUNE TO IT, IT BEHOOVES US TO BEGIN TAKING PRE-DATING REFLECTION MORE SERIOUSLY.

This may include pre- or post-marital counseling once we have found a spouse as well. I have had the great pleasure of working with many young couples during their engagement period and beyond, preparing them for some of the pitfalls that may lie ahead. The freezer should be a period of active reflection, rather than a period of cooling off and just passing the time.

---

127    *Mechilta, Shemos* 19.

# THE FLEDGLING COUPLE:
## INSIGHTS INTO CONCURRENTLY HOLDING ON AND LETTING GO

T here is a well-known story about a single man struggling to find a spouse. His main challenge was his insistence that a potential mate agree that his widowed mother live with them. A friend suggested that he speak with the great authority, HaRav Shlomo Zalman Auerbach. The single man shared with the rabbi his delicate predicament. The rabbi validated the man's approach as acceptable. Sometime later, the man met his *bashert*—and she was willing to let Mom live with them. They returned to Rabbi Auerbach for his blessing. Rabbi Auerbach surprisingly called aside the man and told him that he can't live with his mother anymore. The young man was shocked. After all, on the previous visit, the rabbi had supported the idea! The sage explained that he understood the young man's exceptional requirement as a test of sorts, to ensure that the young lady he would marry would be a woman of valor, a woman of kindness. But once he had, in fact, found such a woman, it was imperative for the sake of the marriage—as newlyweds—to find the mother another place to live.

Most newly married couples don't permanently invite parents into their private dwelling in a literal sense, but figuratively, they may bring their parents along for the ride.

## BREAKING FREE

In the national bestseller *The Good Marriage*, Judith Wallerstein and Sandra Blakeslee report that many marriage counselors tell their clients "there are at least six people in every marriage—the couple and both sets of parents."[128] A delicate balance must be struck between maintaining positive and meaningful connection with family of origin, while at the same time not alienating the new spouse and the fledgling marital union.

THERE ARE AT LEAST SIX PEOPLE IN EVERY MARRIAGE–THE COUPLE AND BOTH SETS OF PARENTS.

In his renowned work *The Art of Loving*,[129] Eric Fromm discusses object relations theory[130] and the process of individuation from parents. He explains that ideally we physically separate from our parents, while concurrently bringing them with us in our minds and hearts. In this way, our parents are a support and a significant and influential backdrop throughout our lives.

---

128    Wallerstein and Blakeslee, *The Good Marriage: How and Why Love Lasts* (Grand Central Publishing, 1996), p. 7.

129    Published originally in 1956 by Harper and Row, Inc., p. 10.

130    Object relations theory in psychoanalytic psychology is the process of developing a psyche in relation to others in the environment during childhood. Based on psychodynamic theory, the object relations theory suggests that the way people relate to others and situations in their adult lives is shaped by family experiences during infancy. For example, adults who experienced neglect or abuse in infancy would expect similar behavior from others who remind them of the neglectful or abusive person from their past. These images of people and events turn into *objects* in the subconscious that the person carries into adulthood, and they are used by the subconscious to predict people's behavior in their social relationships and interactions.

## DREAMING OF DADDY

This concept is highlighted in a famous episode in *Parshas Vayeshev*.[131] The wife of Potifar (Potifar was an influential member of Pharoh's cabinet) attempts to seduce Yosef who is working in her home as a servant. This episode takes place soon after his brothers sell Yosef to the Egyptians. Yosef is ultimately saved from *eshet Potifar*'s advances with the help of the image of his father Yaakov, *dmus dyukno shel aviv*,[132] appearing in his mind at the critical moment before sin, preventing the iniquity. Yosef is far away from his home, but yet able to marshal Yaakov's values and spiritual strength when it was most needed.

> *Many years ago, I guided and helped a young couple immediately after their marriage. It seemed that the husband was looking forward to a honeymoon with his new bride. His wife wasn't adverse to the honeymoon, but her family had planned their yearly family vacation and the young lady didn't want to give up on this family time. I empathized with both the young man's disappointment in potentially having his new in-laws intrude on his honeymoon time, and the young women's deep desire to remain attached to her parents and siblings.*

The tensions and conflicts regarding in-laws, parents and families are rampant in many marriages and don't always have easy solutions. Sometimes a young couple is placed in the unenviable position of having to erect boundaries, as the more "mature" parents are oblivious to these considerations and are grasping to hold onto a child. It's a complex dance with competing interests.

Let's try to articulate some foundational principles to protect the marriage and the formation and development of the couple.

---

131   Chap. 39.
132   Rashi, 39:11.

## BUILDING WALLS

We know that Jewish couples stand under a *chuppah* (canopy) during the marriage ceremony.[133] The *chuppah* symbolizes the home and the husband bringing the wife into his material and spiritual domain. Interestingly, the canopy has no walls—just a roof. The task of erecting walls is left to the couple. They must, over the course of their lives together, fill in those walls and thereby fortify their relationship.

> THEY MAY KNOW INTELLECTUALLY THAT THE SPOUSE IS THE TOP PRIORITY, BUT EMOTIONALLY THEY MAY NOT BE THERE YET.

What is challenging is that this process takes time. Early on, the couple is certainly more connected to their family of origin than to each other. They may know intellectually that the spouse is the top priority, but emotionally they may not be there yet. The ideal at this early stage is to communicate the desire and goal to deepen the marriage while, at the same time, not transition too quickly. It may even be sensible to have designated times with family, while protecting some time just for the couple alone.

I once heard a therapist in one of my graduate courses share the profound insight that "life is long." Things don't happen immediately and patience is essential to happiness. One needs to have an eye on the long term and realize that even five years in the scope of what will hopefully be a life-long commitment isn't really entirely significant. Problem is, we are often caught in the particular moment and choose to live in a vacuum, adding anguish and frustration to our existence.

## MONEY AND CONTROL

When there is extreme difficulty separating or creating healthy space from a family of origin, it may reflect resistance to transitioning fully into adulthood by one—or both—members of the couple. In our religious communities, where couples often marry young, this is a most serious predicament. It is exacerbated when children are still relying on parents

---

133    See a nice article by Rabbi Maurice Lamm on *chuppah* at chabad.org.

for financial support. As I once heard expressed, *"Ba'al meah, ba'al deah,"* or not as subtly, "The one who pays, says."[134]

Moreover, the important Torah precept of *kibbud av v'eim*[135] adds complexity and sometimes even guilt when attempting to develop as a couple. Despite these challenges, the couple must understand that their goal is to be moving toward adulthood and independence both emotionally and financially. At the same time, they must always remain cognizant of their parents' contribution in enabling them to build their new life together.

Money in marriage is itself a very interesting topic. Many people have very deep emotional issues relating to money. I once observed an elderly woman who didn't trust her own children with her money. She was ill and she thought they were trying to steal from her. I also heard of a man who raised millions for Jewish institutions but was careful to only pass it on to the organizations in small doses. He explained that if he provided lump sum payments, they wouldn't need or value him as much. Money and control are fundamentally and intrinsically linked.[136]

## TRUST ME!

Another challenge for the newly married couple is building trust. Young women in particular often confide in their mothers—sometimes numerous times a day. It is vital for the husband to feel that his confidences are

---

134    This reminds me of a young man who had returned from a year of study in Israel and was very excited about his newfound relationship with G-d. He shared with his mother that he was a full-fledged *eved Hashem*, or servant of G-d. The mother responded rather dismissively when not enjoying the direction of the conversation (a subsequent year of study in Israel) by saying, "You're not an *eved Hashem*, you're an *eved Imma*." She meant to say, I pay the bills and therefore I will decide.

135    *Yisro* 20:12.

136    What is so tricky about this reality is that it flies in the face of a Torah-true *hashkafah*. A person ideally is a *ba'al chesed* and *ba'al tzedakah* who gives freely of his bounty and doesn't use it as leverage. Chazal teach us that one should be satisfied with his lot in life and not aspire toward great material wealth. In fact, if a person has what he needs today, he shouldn't exhaust energy worrying about having enough for tomorrow. So many of us are obsessed and controlled by money and impressed with wealth. So many decisions and stresses hinge on money, including *shidduchim*, choice of profession and *aliyah* to name just a few.

being preserved and that his mother-in-law doesn't know every detail of his married life. The same is true vis-à-vis the boy with his parents. Clear boundaries should be delineated and communicated between the couple as to what is appropriate to repeat and what should remain private.

Even as a couple establishes their independence from their families of origin, they still must come together and form a dynamic "dyad." There are two components to this process. I would posit that it echoes the maxim, "*Sur me-ra v'aseh tov*—Avoid evil and attempt good."[137] I don't mean to suggest that the family of origin is "evil," quite the contrary; rather, the child must ensure that there is nothing, not even family, intruding on the new relationship.

## MERGING AND BREAKING DOWN WALLS

Removing possible impediments is necessary, but not sufficient. The next step involves breaking selfish patterns of behavior and the exclusive focus on self. Rabbi Yosef Soloveitchik introduced a beautiful formulation for the concept of parallel constructs in prayer.[138] There is the individual model as well as the communal model. His formulation is "*tefillah b'tzibbur*" and "*tefillat ha-tzibbur*." We pray individually within the framework and context of community and we then repeat the prayer as a communal offering, one representative on behalf of the whole. Similarly, a newly married couple must have individual space for themselves, while at the same time bringing that nurtured self into the couple to create something bigger.

## I, THOU AND WE

Each marital decision must reflect this model of balancing personal needs and what is good for the marriage. One spouse may prefer to spend a holiday with family, but the marriage would be better served spending it at home or with the other's family. That's why marital therapy is

---

137    *Tehillim* 34.
138    Rabbi Hershel Schachter, *Nefesh HaRav* (1994), 123.

more complex than individual work. The client is the marriage as a whole, rather than the two individuals.

This tension sheds light on an idea I heard many years back in the name of Rabbi Shlomo Wolbe.[139] The first year of marriage, which is of great legal and philosophical religious significance, is not a distinct quantitative period, but rather a conceptual qualitative experience that may take many years to complete. This reflects the dual nature and challenge of marriage—letting go slowly of the past and reconstructing it to coincide and overlap with one's future as a married couple.

## IN-LAWS AND OUT-LAWS

A word of advice for parents: Not every parent is emotionally capable of treating a child-in-law like an actual child. It isn't uncommon for children-in-law to be confounded by what to call their in-laws.[140] A parent ideally should try to make their child-in-law as comfortable as possible. This includes showering the same love and kindness one would provide to one's own child. Parents need to be sensitive to the critical role that they play in the formative stages of their children's marriages. They have the ability to lend support and to give space or to be intrusive and domineering. There is no doubt that the parents may

> NOT EVERY PARENT IS EMOTIONALLY CAPABLE OF TREATING A CHILD-IN-LAW LIKE AN ACTUAL CHILD.

> PARENTS AS A WHOLE NEED TO HAVE MORE CONFIDENCE IN THEIR PARENTING SKILLS.

---

139    Found toward the end of *Ma'amarei Hadrachah L'chasanim* of Rabbi Wolbe, 1999.

140    There is often discomfort in the broaching of this sensitive topic. Sometimes, parents don't want to be called Mom and Dad or derivatives of such by a child-in-law, while some in-law children feel that using these names for in-laws is an affront to their own parents. This topic like many others requires delicate exploration. I have seen that over time, even those with hesitation grow into things and become more comfortable, as expressed by the rabbinic maxim, "*Acharei ha-peulos nimshachos ha-levavos*—The heart will follow the deed." I once heard a story of a young man who had anxiety while telling his wife that he loved her. He shared with his *rebbi* that he didn't always feel it each time he said it. The *rebbi* gave him this same advice—keep at it, eventually or at least sometimes, you will actually feel it.

have mixed emotions about their child transitioning to this new stage in life, but they need to be cognizant and self-aware. Parents as a whole should have more confidence in their parenting skills. They must trust they have done an adequate job instilling within their child good sound judgment. If their beloved child has made this selection, it is most likely a reflection of insights gleaned from the family of origin during many years of profound influence, sensitivity and exceptional caring, preparing them for this transition to adulthood.

# MEN ARE FROM MINSK, WOMEN ARE FROM VILNA

**T**here is a story about a husband who is always accumulating "stuff" and it irritates his wife. One day, Mr. Collector arrives home with a beautiful yacht that he places on the front lawn. His wife is beside herself and they spiral into the usual argument about how his stuff takes up too much space. To assuage her feelings, he tells her he is honoring her with the naming of the yacht. He is off to do some shopping to buy some trinkets for his great new acquisition, and he anxiously anticipates the name she will come up with. When he returns home, he notices in big bold black lettering the new name of the yacht. It says "FOR SALE"!

## MISSION AND VISION

When a couple begins dating, shared life goals are certainly an important criterion for embarking upon a healthy, fulfilling marriage. If they have very different visions of happiness and direction, they are better off marrying someone more aligned with their values. Different life goals is a recipe for a difficult and unfulfilling marriage. Sometimes, a couple can marry and have shared values, but very different ways of expressing or arriving at those values. They are then left to negotiate an equilibrium that works for both of them and leaves them both feeling validated and satisfied.

> IF THEY HAVE VERY DIFFERENT VISIONS OF HAPPINESS AND DIRECTION, THEY ARE BETTER OFF MARRYING SOMEONE MORE ALIGNED WITH THEIR VALUES.

## THE PROVERBIAL SHALOM BAYIS

*Shalom bayis* is a term bantered about with a diversity of meaning.[141] We assume it to mean marital harmony or ensuring a peaceful home. The question is, who is primarily responsible for ensuring this lofty marital goal? The *midrash* says that "*Ishah kesheirah osah retzon ba'alah*—A good Jewish woman listens to or performs the will of her husband."[142] On the other hand, when I was in *shidduchim*, a wise *shadchan*[143] once said to me, "A happy wife is a happy life." Interestingly, a recently divorced man quoted the same mantra to me. Chazal also say that a man without a wife lacks joy and multitudes of other *brachah*,[144] thereby implying great value in ensuring a wife's happiness as she holds the key to multiple portals of his own success.

> WHEN I WAS IN *SHIDDUCHIM*, A WISE *SHADCHAN* ONCE SAID TO ME "A HAPPY WIFE IS A HAPPY LIFE." INTERESTINGLY, A RECENTLY DIVORCED MAN QUOTED THE SAME MANTRA TO ME.

---

141    *Shabbos* 23b.
142    Midrash, *Shoftim* 5.
143    Rebbetzin Judy Young, *z"l*, daughter of Rabbi Maurice Lamm.
144    *Yevamos* 62b.

## KEEPING SCORE

When I work with couples, I often reference the point system established by my good friend and college roommate.[145] He argued that most things aren't of great significance and aren't worth many points. Don't sweat or waste energy on the small stuff. Make sure to give in on those small things and save your points for when you really need them. Only request when it is a big value or ticket item and not before. The goal is to focus on the quality of the issue and thereby "lose" most of the time. This approach builds or makes deposits for when an issue is critical for you.[146] If it ranks above an eight out of ten for you, only then assert yourself. Hopefully, there will usually be different scales of importance of things between a couple and they will be able to negotiate peacefully through various potential disagreements.

If only life translated so simply! Sometimes, the debate has great value to both parties and is of high value to each partner. The stakes are at times extremely high and it is impossible for both sides to get their way.

## A SHOCKING CONCEPT

My Rosh Yeshiva, Rabbi Yaakov Friedman of Birchas Mordechai in Beitar Illit, says over in his *chassan schmooze* that *shalom bayis* is ultimately and primarily the *man's* responsibility.[147] He quotes from Rabbi Shlomo Wolbe that even in the most trying of circumstances, when a wife has mental illness, the husband still has the ability to set a harmonious tone by doing his part and being most sensitive to the needs of his

> THE MESSAGE IS TO FOCUS ON YOUR PART AND NOT FIXATE ON THE FLAWS OF THE SIGNIFICANT OTHER.

---

145    Rabbi Eli Reich of Sha'alvim.

146    Stephen Covey makes reference to the concept of deposits and withdrawals in the realm of relationships in his famous best-selling book, *The Seven Habits of Highly Effective People.*

147    There is a nice *kuntras* published in 2006 available at the yeshiva office entitled *Yesodos B'shalom Bayis.*

wife.[148] The message is to focus on your part and not fixate on the flaws of the significant other. Her behavior can never be an excuse for his neglect or vindictiveness.

At times, a critical decision is objectively for the benefit of the family unit and the marriage and therefore the logical choice, and yet is still difficult for the wife to accept. I know of a situation where a family was forced to move across the country for *parnassah* reasons. The wife understood intellectually that the husband must be able to support her, however, emotionally the move was overwhelming and very difficult for her. He had hoped for her acquiescence and unwavering support and it just wasn't forthcoming. Instead, despite his best efforts to be responsible, he faced great resistance. In this difficult scenario for both participants, it is the husband who needs to be able to keep his emotions in check and realize the challenges his wife faces.

## SCIENTIFICALLY DOCUMENTED DIFFERENCES

I hate to stereotype as there are always exceptions to every rule, but in 2009, the *British Journal of Psychology* had a scientific study that claimed men are better seeing things in the distance while women are better at focusing at close range. The study posited that this was due to brain evolution within genders varying over time.[149] I would posit that if it is true

---

148    This was even after all the professionals agreed that all the problems emanated from her difficult childhood and upbringing.

149    Published July 30, 2009. Helen Stancey at Hammersmith & West London College demonstrated that men and women used a laser pointer to mark the midpoint of lines on a piece of paper within hand's reach (50 cm away) and again beyond hand's reach (100 cm away). The place where the twenty-four women and twenty-four men pointed to was marked, and the distance from their mark to the actual midpoint was measured to judge their accuracy.

Men were found to be more accurate than women at marking the middle of lines when the target was far away as compared to when it was close by. However, women showed the opposite pattern; they were more accurate at finding the midpoint of the line when the target was close to them as compared to when it was further away. Stancey concluded: "Evidence already exists that separate pathways in the brain process visual information from near and far space. Our results suggest that the near pathway is favoured in women and the far pathway is favoured in men. These sex differences in visual processing may be a result of our hunter-gatherer evolutionary legacy. As the predominant gatherers, women

that women are more detail-oriented or focus more carefully and intensely (while men see the bigger picture more accurately), then by extension, transition is harder for them. They by nature are fixated on the various particulars of any transition—both on what is being left behind and on the new adjustments ahead. The husband need not interpret resistance as non-compliance with his wishes; but rather as having greater difficulty with adjusting to the new realities on the ground. It is the responsibility of the husband to be attuned to his wife's reactions, understand their origins and control his frustrations.

## FLEXIBILITY VS. INTRACTABILITY

An *adam gadol* didn't sight this study to me, but would often share in conversation with me that it is harder for women by their nature to bend or be flexible. I never fully understood why he said this or how he knew this, and (from my limited perspective) he had a wife who was very devoted to his will, but the message was clear. The man must try and be as flexible as possible as by nature it is harder for most women to do so.

## MONEY AND SUBMISSION

I have seen on occasion a phenomenon where some men look for the type of women in *shidduchim* who will be entirely focused on their concerns and ambitions. The women's sole responsibility in marriage is to be the proverbial *ishah kesheirah*. I have seen this more amongst affluent men who in return will take care of "everything else." This model can certainly work, though it may defeat the larger marital function of perfecting, refining and correcting *middos* and striving for the oneness and partnership that Hashem desires we glean from marriage.

I recall once hearing in a *shiur* that marriage is a significant tool

> BY LEARNING TO SUBMIT ONE'S WILL TO ANOTHER, TO THAT OF ONE'S PARTNER, IT IS THEN AN EASIER TRANSITION TO SUBMITTING TO A HIGHER DIVINE WILL.

would have needed to work well in near space, whereas the prey for (predominantly male) hunters would have been in far space."

in *avodas Hashem*. By learning to submit one's will to another, to that of one's partner, it is then an easier transition to submitting to a higher Divine will. "*Bitul*" or self-nullification and abnegation is fundamental in having harmonious relationships *bein adam laMakom* and *lachaveiro*.

## AWARENESS AND DRIVE

The salient point is a man can move forward with his ambitious plans in life even without the full acquiescence of his wife. However, it is naive and insensitive of him to expect her to just fall in line and do his bidding in most circumstances, especially when it is difficult and possibly transformational.

> IT IS NAIVE AND INSENSITIVE OF HIM TO EXPECT HER TO JUST FALL IN LINE AND DO HIS BIDDING IN MOST CIRCUMSTANCES, ESPECIALLY WHEN IT IS DIFFICULT AND POSSIBLY TRANSFORMATIONAL.

This tension or dialectic, requires of the husband maximal efforts to listen, validate and acknowledge her sincere concerns and reservations. With such devotion and attention, he may sometimes even change course. If he can venture to enter her emotional universe, it will go a long way to securing his own happiness.

## THE SECRET OF SUCCESS

A man who suffers from a difficult wife likely hasn't invested enough or done the legwork he needs to do. It is rare to find a woman who resists a husband who is committed to her feelings and needs even when not doing exactly what she wants. This might be the deeper meaning to the *midrash* cited earlier of *ishah kesheirah osah retzon ba'alah*—she does it less begrudgingly when she feels cared about and not dismissed while cajoled concurrently by his cold or forceful logic. Through his intensive sensitivity and deftness of touch, she is now *kesheirah*, i.e.,

> MEN HAVE THE OPPORTUNITY AND CHALLENGE TO SET A CONTEXT AND BACKDROP IN THE HOME WHERE A WOMAN CAN BE CONVINCED AND FEEL SECURE THAT HER HUSBAND ALWAYS WANTS WHAT IS ULTIMATELY BEST FOR HER.

*muchshar*, or prepared, to do his bidding without feelings of alienation. This singular focus on her emotional realities ensures her happiness and by extension his own. Men have the opportunity and challenge to set a context and backdrop in the home where a woman can be convinced and feel secure that her husband always wants what is ultimately best for her.

## A NOT-SO-FUNNY JOKE

I conclude with this short anecdote.

> *A woman arrives in therapy and receives a compelling compliment from the female therapist. The therapist, observing tangible relief and release in her client, turns to the husband and admonishes him by remarking that this type of positive affirmation is what she needed all along. The husband without even thinking remarks, I can bring her here to therapy on Monday and Wednesday but on Fridays, I have a chavrusa!*

Many of us men just don't get it! We are cozily tucked away in Minsk, while our beloved wives are most comfortable in Vilna. We must study our own personal *sugyos* of *nashim* and *ishus* in great depth with all the accompanying *lomdus* to ensure we get things right—and break what is at times our less delicate natures. Although not always natural, this focus and perspective is what will truly ensure that the famous words of the *midrash* about *ishah kesheirah* resonate in each of our homes and our lives.

# SECTION FIVE

Being Present and

Paying Attention

# BEING IN THE MOMENT

**T**here is a famous sports mantra that the most important game is the game we are currently playing. Irrelevant of the team in front of them, the very best teams treat every game like it is a "one-game season." This approach and attitude parallels a powerful realization of the Jewish people as we accepted the Torah on Har Sinai.

**THE MOST IMPORTANT GAME IS THE GAME WE ARE CURRENTLY PLAYING.**

When we were offered the Torah on Har Sinai, our collective response was "*Na'aseh v'nishma*—We will do, and (only after) will we come to understand."[150]

## LIFE AS A LADDER

Rebbe Nachman of Breslov explains that *na'aseh* is a commitment to stay focused on the immediate present.[151] *Nishma*, by contrast, represents a world currently beyond the realm of our ability. The Jewish

---

150    *Mishpatim* 24:7.
151    *Likutei Moharan I*, 22.10.

people accepted responsibility for the present, recognizing that each focused act, a *na'aseh*, is the only path toward arriving upon the cusp of *nishma*, something that was ungraspable at an earlier point in time. A Jew aspires for spiritual transcendence, but only reaches it through the steady performance of everyday activities.

Rebbe Nachman further elucidates this point by highlighting a dichotomy between Torah and *tefillah* (prayer). Torah represents the *na'aseh*, the law that we are currently practicing. *Tefillah* is the *nishma*, representing our longing for something deeper and better in the future. Our daily prayers reflect this concept with supplications filled with anticipation for the return of the Divine presence to Zion and the resurrection of the dead.

Interestingly, Rebbe Nachman's entire work, *Likutei Moharan*, is structured in patterns of learning and prayer. First, Rebbe Nachman communicates his ideas, the Torah—the *na'aseh*. Then, he concretizes these thoughts with poetic expressions of prayer (the *nishma*), asking Hashem for guidance to implement these ideas in the future.

## JEWISH JOURNEY

The task of every Jew is to take life a step at a time and remain focused on the *na'aseh*. As each subsequent *na'aseh* is conquered, we magically arrive at the *nishma*, once considered beyond our reach.

There is a book by Mihaly Csikszentmihalyi, *Finding Flow—The Psychology of Engagement with Everyday Life*,[152] that has been well received in the self-help community. The book details how to reach a state of "effortless concentration," enabling a person to fully maximize and capitalize upon any particular moment in time. He instructs his readers:

> Imagine that you are skiing down a slope and your full attention is focused on the movements of your body, the position of the skis, the air whistling past your face, and the snow-shrouded

---

152    Harper Collins Publishers Inc., 1997.

trees running by. There is no room in your awareness for conflicts or contradictions; you know that a distracting thought or
emotion might get you buried face down in the snow. The run is
so perfect that you want it to last forever.

If skiing does not mean much to you, this complete immer-
sion in an experience could occur while you are singing in a
choir, dancing, playing bridge or reading a good book. If you
love your job, it could happen during a complicated surgical operation or a close business deal. It may occur in a social interaction, when talking with a good friend, or while playing with a
baby. Moments such as these provide flashes of intense living
against the dull background of everyday life.[153]

Csikszentmihalyi is communicating that the *nishma* must, at first, be
neglected. Being in the moment is all about the *na'aseh*, the immediate
challenge before you. "Finding flow" entails being fully engaged in the
moment.

## THE VASTNESS OF IT ALL

Upon receiving the profundity of the Torah, the Jewish nation, as one,
proclaims, "*Na'aseh v'nishma.*" They
recognize that the Ten Commandments are really just the tip of the
iceberg of new obligations and responsibilities redefining their very
essence and existence. Their im-
mediate response reflects an understanding that to succeed in this new
endeavor, they must first act. They must be focused on the moment and
be attentive to whichever commandment lies before them. The method
toward "conquering" the entire corpus of law and ethical imperatives that
they have received is ... one *na'aseh* at a time.

THEY RECOGNIZE THAT THE TEN
COMMANDMENTS ARE REALLY JUST
THE TIP OF THE ICEBERG OF NEW
OBLIGATIONS AND RESPONSIBILITIES
REDEFINING THEIR VERY ESSENCE
AND EXISTENCE.

---

153    P. 29.

## ENDLESS DISTRACTIONS

There is an expression: "Yesterday is history, tomorrow is a mystery and today is a gift; that's why it's called the present."[154]

Our "present" is one of the most distracting periods in history. The endless technological gadgets and the immense pressures to keep pace in an ever-sophisticated environment almost demand that we focus on too much at any given time. The challenge is to remain committed to the *na'aseh* in every given moment. With this single-minded determination in as many moments of life as possible, we will be able to transition from the *na'aseh* into a most historic *nishma*. Every Jew has immense spiritual potential, our personal *nishma*. These can be accessed only through perpetual unadulterated emphasis on the *na'aseh* of everyday experience.

---

154    William Aloysius Keane, better known as Bil Keane, was an American cartoonist most notable for his work on the long-running newspaper comic, *The Family Circus*.

# SPIRITUAL LESSONS
# ON THE HIGH SEAS

Chazal teach, "*Mitzvah goreres mitzvah*—One good deed or thing leads to another."[155] A couple of Pesachs ago, I served as scholar-in-residence in Florida at an upscale program. I connected and befriended one of the participants and he suggested to me that I'd be a good fit as a scholar on a summer cruise. With his recommendation, I was ultimately invited on a cruise to the Greek Islands. I had never been on a cruise ship before and it was a unique and exhilarating opportunity. I was a bit nervous about being "out at sea," but thankfully it proved mostly to be a smooth ride. The ship, called the *Costa Fascinosa*, holds approximately 3,800 people. Our group was carved out within the larger group and comprised 120 participants.

With my wife by my side, my role was to provide the spiritual nourishment to complement the plentiful physical sustenance that was available for the guests to enjoy. Things started off a bit slowly. I was competing with

---

155    *Avos* 4:2.

all sorts of exciting cruise ship activities and had a paltry turnout for my initial lecture. Thankfully, the handful of participants at this lecture enjoyed, including the Kosherica owner, Yehuda Shiffman, and they helped promote the learning program going forward. Attendance

> MY ROLE WAS TO PROVIDE THE SPIRITUAL NOURISHMENT TO COMPLEMENT THE PLENTIFUL PHYSICAL SUSTENANCE THAT WAS AVAILABLE FOR THE GUESTS TO ENJOY.

grew exponentially throughout the week. Through my teaching and interacting with people at meals, I cultivated many new, meaningful relationships.

## SHARING FAVORITES

In our home, we have an exercise where we ask our children on Sunday evenings to share with us the best part of their day. Interestingly, one of my kids (who is a little sensitive or, as he likes to say, "sensible") usually decides to share the worst or most hurtful part of his day. We encourage this as well, as it is important to

> IN OUR HOME, WE HAVE AN EXERCISE WHERE WE ASK OUR CHILDREN ON SUNDAY EVENINGS TO SHARE WITH US THE BEST PART OF THEIR DAY.

be comfortable sharing and validating all feelings, both positive and negative. This serves as meaningful family interaction and bonding time, as well as challenges the children to concretize their feelings and experiences.

Upon my return from the cruise (and in this spirit), I was asked by my children what my favorite part of the cruise was. I told them I loved the various beautiful stops we made. It was breathtaking to visit places such as Venice, Italy, Santorini, Greece and Dubrovnik, Croatia to name just a few ports we visited. However, this wasn't the most profound or meaningful aspect of the trip by any stretch.

## A JEWISH UNITED NATIONS

We are all familiar with the United Nations (UN). As supporters of Israel, we may even be a bit too familiar in a negative sense. In theory, if not in practice, the purpose of an organization to promote international cooperation is a forum to work together to address world problems and issues. It creates context to bind peoples of all backgrounds together in their shared human experience.

The cruise was, in a way, a "United Nations of the Jewish world." Within our relatively small group were guests from Mexico, Panama, Brazil, Italy, England, Switzerland, Russia, Israel and the United States. There was great diversity within the United States group as well, representing states such as Florida, California, Virginia, Connecticut, Michigan, New York and Illinois. Some of the guests were not even fluent in English and I had ample opportunity to brush up on my Hebrew speaking skills when I made announcements in shul or in conversation. One guest was an eighty-five-year-old lady from Israel accompanied by her children and grandchildren. There was even a group of three female friends who each brought along a granddaughter. There was also a newly minted couple celebrating their honeymoon, and a world-renowned Jewish philanthropist.

> THE CRUISE WAS, IN A WAY, A "UNITED NATIONS OF THE JEWISH WORLD."

## A SOCIAL ANIMAL

I love interacting with people. This is probably a major reason I entered the rabbinate, a (seriously) people-oriented profession. When I (often) return late from a shul meeting, *minyan* or class, my daughter excitedly proclaims with a twinkle in her eye, "Abba, you are such a schmoozer!" Unfortunately for me, my wife isn't always as appreciative.

> WHEN I (OFTEN) RETURN LATE FROM A SHUL MEETING, *MINYAN* OR CLASS, MY DAUGHTER EXCITEDLY PROCLAIMS WITH A TWINKLE IN HER EYE, "ABBA, YOU ARE SUCH A SCHMOOZER!"

For a schmoozer like myself, the cruise ship was a paradise of sorts. An opportunity for building relationships, exploring diverse Jewish communities and confronting issues of challenge that bind us together. It represented what the United Nations should really be about.

When I addressed the *shidduch* crisis at the Friday night *oneg*, it was fascinating to hear the varying perspectives and sets of circumstances in different places. The lady from Mexico who married at seventeen, the man from Europe with the older single son with *parnassah* exclusively in his hometown and the girl who is a *ba'alas teshuvah* without family "connections."[156] I stressed to my kids that most certainly, the experience of being at sea while exposed to Jews of different varieties and flavors was a highlight of the vacation.

## THE BEST PART

The final best part of the cruise was very personal and not really age appropriate for my children. It happened Shabbos afternoon as I sat on the top deck and peered out toward the water. We were sailing from Greece toward Croatia, but there was no land in sight. All there was to see for miles on end, in every direction, was perfectly blue water and the clear blue skies. The beauty and serenity was just impossible to describe. My wife had left the cruise for Shabbos and I was experiencing this moment alone.

There is something scary about being "alone," or by oneself. Somebody once said to me that they are alone, but they aren't lonely. In my training as a marital therapist, I was taught that everybody is alone, and that even the very best marriages have moments when each participant feels truly alone. The instructor posited

> THERE IS SOMETHING SCARY ABOUT BEING "ALONE," OR BY ONESELF.

that there are certain things that we just do alone and that nobody else, not even the most committed spouse, can relate to.

He then said, "Everybody dies alone." No matter how connected we are to people down here on earth, we transition or move on to the next world alone. The expression goes regarding material possessions that we "can't take them with us."[157] We also can't take people with us and there are aspects of life that we must get comfortable experiencing alone. May-

---

156    This young woman reached out to me shortly after from across the ocean to share the wonderful news of her engagement.

157    My grandfather would often use this line when soliciting funds for his synagogue.

be with support, maybe alongside others, but ultimately alone. A social being like myself may have greater difficulty than others integrating this reality. It is scary to be alone without social interaction and support, and the specter of ultimate death and being all-alone is daunting.

## THE WORLD TO COME–OLAM HABA

It was in that very moment where I think I experienced for the first time in my life the absolute reality of *Olam Haba*, the World to Come. I'm a devoted Jew who always believed in the next world, but on that afternoon it was truly tangible, as if the sky had come down and touched the earth. The universe is so vast and I, but a small speck in the grand cosmos, felt with absolute certainty that there is something out there much bigger than what I was experiencing in front of me. As I stood confronting the vastness and endlessness of the blue sea, I knew absolutely that there was so much more beyond as well. It was like a *kal vachomer*, a fortiori of sorts. If Hashem made all this, then He certainly is capable of so much more. It was a transformative moment that brought tears to my eyes, a genuine religious experience on the Aegean Sea that I briefly referenced in my lecture later that afternoon.

> THE UNIVERSE IS SO VAST AND I, BUT A SMALL SPECK IN THE GRAND COSMOS, FELT WITH ABSOLUTE CERTAINTY THAT THERE IS SOMETHING OUT THERE MUCH BIGGER THAN WHAT I WAS EXPERIENCING IN FRONT OF ME.

## SEEING THE FUTURE

The daily monotony of life can be limiting and cause us to constrict rather than expand. It is hard to think big and be "big Jews" when surrounded by our usual environs. A vacation or break is often warranted to reorient ourselves and help us see a bigger picture. I sensed from many of my traveling companions that the cruise was "just what

> I SENSED FROM MANY OF MY TRAVELING COMPANIONS THAT THE CRUISE WAS "JUST WHAT THE DOCTOR ORDERED" FOR A RANGE OF PERSONAL MALADIES AND STRESSES.

the doctor ordered" for a range of personal maladies and stresses. Yet, I would have never anticipated the gift of feeling but for a fleeting moment the concept of *"olamecha yeru bechayecha,"*[158] a taste of the World to Come, in the most tangible way that I had ever felt it.

Death is about faith, because there is no other way to deal with its starkness and enormous implications. Some of us are more aware of it and many of us push it away into the subconscious, but we all will personally encounter it one day. As I am, not so recently, into my forties it looms larger. As I watch my children grow older, bigger and more curious and watch my parents get older as well, it taunts and peeks at me.

> AS I WATCH MY CHILDREN GROW OLDER, BIGGER AND MORE CURIOUS AND WATCH MY PARENTS GET OLDER AS WELL, IT TAUNTS AND PEEKS AT ME.

Death asks us plainly what we have accomplished and how we are spending our time.

> DEATH ASKS US PLAINLY WHAT WE HAVE ACCOMPLISHED AND HOW WE ARE SPENDING OUR TIME.

How I yearn to be able to stare it directly in the eye, knowing it can come at any moment and still fear it not. Death is the great motivator and great equalizer. Thanks to my summer cruise, it is a drop less frightening.

Because even though each of us will experience it alone, there is nothing to really be afraid of. The masterful Master of the Universe awaits each of us on the "other side" to offer a monumental embrace, on hopefully, a job very well done.

---

158    *Berachos* 17a. There is a cute story about a man who leaves *kollel*, feels guilty and conflicted and comes to discuss the decision with Rabbi Aharon Kotler. R' Aharon understood the need to transition and said the man need not worry about his *Olam Haba*, but what would be of his *Olam Hazeh* if he had to spend all his time working? Learning Torah can in fact be a taste of the World to Come in this ephemeral transient world.

# CARPE DIEM

The appropriate response is certainly silence. The problem is that I'm expected to speak. A good rabbi steps up to the plate the Shabbos after a tragedy like the one in Newtown, Connecticut, and provides perspective to his congregation. The gunning down of innocent elementary school children while in school has become not so uncommon in America and concurrently, still so shocking and unexplainable. The fear of these events is very real. In fact, all the doorknobs in my daughters' school have been bolted locked and one must now push forward on the door to open. The thinking being: an additional split second may one day save innocent lives.

## COUNTERINTUITIVE

Many years ago, I was considering a *shidduch* with a young woman who was the child of Holocaust survivors. My potential future in-laws were elderly and were closer in age to my grandparents than my parents. I went to

WHO REALLY KNOWS WHO IS OLD AND WHO IS YOUNG?

ask Rabbi Moshe Shapiro if this was cause for concern. He responded using just six words. *"Mi yodei'a mi zaken u-mi tza'ir?*—Who really knows who is old and who is young?" Subsequently, I realized the poignancy of his statement; R' Moshe had lost a daughter at the tender age of sixteen. When children are murdered, six years old can, in fact, be "very old."

The loss of a child is probably the most painful loss that can be experienced in life. Yaakov Avinu states it clearly when, upon hearing of the loss of Yosef, he refused to be comforted, saying, "For I will go to the grave mourning for my son."[159]

## POWERLESSNESS

When we see pictures of so many pure little children who are no longer with us, besides mourning their loss, we all feel vulnerable. When I walked into my daughter's elementary school the very next week, I couldn't help but worry that such horrors could transpire in Manhattan. In truth, nobody really knows what is coming next. We get lulled into a comfort zone and feel over-confident. An incident like this quickly puts us back in touch with reality.

> *Rabbi Yonasan Eibeshutz was walking in Poland and being tormented by a non-Jewish governor. The man asked the rav where he was going. The rav responded that he did not know. The governor was infuriated as he felt he was being mocked, so he had the rav incarcerated.*
>
> *A few days later, after calming down, the governor went to talk with the rav. The governor commented that he was shocked by the rav's response to his query, as certainly the smartest of the Jews must know to where he is walking! R' Yonasan responded, "You see, I thought I was heading to the study hall, but I ended up in prison. So in truth, I really didn't know to where I was heading."[160]*

I recently had a conversation with a woman who was bemoaning her child's difficult plight in *shidduchim*. She remarked that this is the only realm in her life that she feels she has no control over. She went on to

---

159    *Vayeshev* 37:35.
160    I saw this story in the written lectures of Rabbi Tzvi Meir Silberberg of Jerusalem.

share how every other aspect of life she seems able to maneuver or orchestrate with her talents and skills. I did not have the heart (nor did I think she was open to hearing) how misguided her approach and attitude truly were—in all aspects of life.

We make plans, as we should. We do our best to bring them to reality, as we should.

But we really don't know what the future holds—and have no control over it.[161] (Life is often like planning for Italy and ending up in Holland.)

> WE MAKE PLANS, AS WE SHOULD. WE DO OUR BEST TO BRING THEM TO REALITY, AS WE SHOULD. BUT WE REALLY DON'T KNOW WHAT THE FUTURE HOLDS—AND HAVE NO CONTROL OVER IT.

## NO EXCUSES

This reality of lack of control demands a special life orientation. If we've lived long enough, then we are almost certain to have been blindsided by some life event. One never knows what tomorrow may bring, and therefore it is incumbent upon each of us to live each and every moment to its fullest.

Life's transience, uncertainty and fickleness demand concrete action. Rebbe Nachman of Breslov (who, by the way, died at the age of thirty-eight) stated that "the entire world is a very narrow bridge, and the main thing is not to be afraid at all." The narrow bridge communi-

> THE ENTIRE WORLD IS A VERY NARROW BRIDGE, AND THE MAIN THING IS NOT TO BE AFRAID AT ALL.

cates the dangers of life, but we still must move forward and progress without being paralyzed by fear.

We do not control (nor can we answer) the "why" (*lamah*), but we can control the "what" (*l'mah*).[162]

We can choose to respond to tragedy by stepping up and living our

---

161  There is a Yiddish expression that "*man tracht v'Gut lacht*," that man works hard and G-d just laughs at us.

162  Rabbi Soloveichik in *Kol Dodi Dofek* discusses the response to tragedy in the following way: Our response is not "Why?" but rather, "For what purpose?" or "Where do we go from here?" So many amazing *chesed* organizations in Israel and abroad were offshoots or derivatives of tragedies that people turned into opportunities to help others in need.

lives to the fullest. It is not the time to cower and, therefore, fall short of what we are destined to become.

## OVERLAPPING WORLDS

Another fundamental response to tragedy is the realization (and internal concretization) of the realities of *techiyas ha-meisim* and the World to Come as basic, immutable tenets of our faith. Those who have experienced the loss of a loved one are often more in tune with these principles.

Rabbi Aryeh Kaplan[163] writes that our transition to the next world is similar to a baby transitioning from the world of souls into this physical world. Initially it is dark and scary, but ultimately the baby is welcomed into the light, greeted with open arms, and comforted. In the end, we all will be comforted and reunited with our loved ones.

Additionally, the institutions of *Yizkor* and *yahrtzeit* are meant to keep us connected with the deceased while they are not physically present. On the Festivals, when we reach elevated spiritual heights, we are more able to connect with the world of the *neshamos,* and therefore we recite *Yizkor* to invoke the memory of departed loved ones. On a *yahrtzeit*, we daven and do *mitzvos* in their merit, reflecting our belief that what we do indeed impacts their reality in the World to Come. Furthermore, we ask at a funeral that the departed serve as a *meilitz yosher*, or conduit, for us. These complex aspects of our observance reflect our deepest belief that our loved ones are "alive and well" and "with us" in spirit though not in the form we once knew.

> THESE COMPLEX ASPECTS OF OUR OBSERVANCE REFLECT OUR DEEPEST BELIEF THAT OUR LOVED ONES ARE "ALIVE AND WELL" AND "WITH US" IN SPIRIT THOUGH NOT IN THE FORM WE ONCE KNEW.

## ACCOMPLISHMENT FOR THEM AND US

Rabbi Avraham Yitzchak Hakohen Kook writes that the "purely righteous

---

163    Last essay in his book *Encounters*.

do not complain about wickedness, rather they add righteousness."[164] I once heard about a man who authored over a hundred books in his lifetime. When asked how he was so prolific, he shared that in his youth his twin brother had suddenly passed away, and he had always felt the burden to accomplish for both of them.

This is echoed in the explanation that some give for the recitation of *Kaddish* upon the loss of a loved one. Every Jew is a walking, breathing *Kiddush Hashem*. When such a person is removed from the world, we must "replace" him or her by reciting the *Kaddish,* which brings glory to Hashem and fills that gaping void.[165]

## ARE WE ALL TERMINALLY ILL?

I end with an apocryphal story about a baby born with a terminal illness. The doctors inform the parents that despite all the vast medical research, there is no cure for this unique illness. When the parents inquire as to the name of the illness, they are told that it's called Life.[166]

Fortunately, we all have this illness of Life, but we must remind ourselves each day that it will not last forever. Let us be galvanized to seize the day—or as they say in Latin, "carpe diem"—and transform our ultimate fate into our eternal destiny.

---

164    *Arpeli Tohar*, p. 39.
165    Heard from Rabbi Yissocher Frand of Ner Yisroel in Baltimore.
166    Heard from Rabbi Zev Leff.

# A TINY MENORAH
# SHINES IN THE WHITE
# HOUSE RED ROOM

The juxtaposition of the two Chanukah celebrations was striking. Zos Chanukah,[167] the eighth and final day, is a time of sublime spiritual potential.

For me, it began with the lighting of the famed menorah of the Maggid of Kozhnitz[168] by Rabbi Shimshon Sternberg,

---

167    The eighth day of Chanukah is known as Zos Chanukah (in earlier times it was called Chanukas Hamizbe'ach) named for the Torah portion we read. The day is *mesugal* (appropriate) for one to daven for barren women to have children, for a *refuah sheleimah* and for one to be blessed with increased *parnassah*.

168    The menorah originally belonged to the Kozhnitzer Maggid, Rabbi Yisrael Hopstein, a disciple of Rebbe Elimelech of Lizhensk who has been described as one of the three founding fathers of chassidism in Poland. The story is told that the Rebbe's daughter, Perela, had lost several children and the Kozhnitzer beseeched the *gedolim* of his time to bless his daughter with healthy children. The Berditchever Rebbe came to the Kozhnitzer Maggid and asked

the Kozhnitzer Rebbe of Tel Aviv, and a product of the Upper West Side. An overflow crowd representing the entire spectrum of the Upper West Side community, including many of its *rabbanim*, gathered to experience this once-a-year lighting of a menorah.

## A BIT COUNTERINTUITIVE

Before lighting, the Rebbe said that he had overheard people commenting on the tiny size of the menorah. He explained that people would expect a Rebbe to have a grandiose and ostentatious menorah, but, in fact, this tiny menorah is perfectly suited for its purpose. The light of the menorah is symbolic of the inner world of the Jew, and that inner sanctum is modest and private, enabling an inverse impact in the higher realms and spheres of existence. This special menorah also had a wall behind it, which reflects this inner focus.

THE LIGHT OF THE MENORAH IS SYMBOLIC OF THE INNER WORLD OF THE JEW, AND THAT INNER SANCTUM IS MODEST AND PRIVATE, ENABLING AN INVERSE IMPACT IN THE HIGHER REALMS AND SPHERES OF EXISTENCE.

## NAPOLEON AND THE MAGGID

The Rebbe commented that a great *tzaddik* like his holy ancestor could influence the cosmos while sitting in his tiny room. His family, he noted, owned letters from Napoleon Bonaparte asking the Maggid of Kozhnitz to pray for his military

EVEN A NON-JEWISH GENERAL UNDERSTOOD THE POWER OF THE SPIRITUAL FLAME OF A MODEST AND UNASSUMING HOLY YID.

him for his precious, heirloom menorah and upon receiving the prized menorah, the Berditchever Rebbe pronounced it as a wedding gift to the as yet unborn son of the Maggid's daughter, Perela. The Berditchiver's words were fulfilled and years later the menorah was given to that same child upon his wedding. The menorah was eventually returned to the Kozhnitzer Maggid and it was passed down from generation to generation, with stories of miraculous happenings through the menorah continuing to be told until today.

success.[169] Even a non-Jewish general understood the power of the spiritual flame of a modest and unassuming holy *Yid*.

These words of the Rebbe echoed what Rabbi Shlomo Wolbe writes in the introduction to his classic *Alei Shur*: Yosef haTzaddik was so beautiful that women would walk on walls to steal a glimpse at him—*bnos tza'adah alei shur*.[170] Rabbi Wolbe explains that the wall symbolizes the divide between the external focus of society at large and the internal world of the yeshiva. His *sefer* is intended to give the striving *ben Torah* a glimpse into the vast potential of this inner world, a world of spiritual grandeur.

## DAVENING IN THE WHITE HOUSE

The morning after this meaningful event, my wife and I embarked on a journey to Washington, D.C. to attend President Obama's fifth annual White House Chanukah party. As we stood in line outside the White House waiting to pass security, we met a couple and exchanged pleasantries. The husband mentioned that he was invited because he is an avid Judaica collector and had donated a unique Statue of Liberty menorah crafted by a Holocaust survivor for the White House ceremony.

As Professor Alan Dershowitz of Harvard Law School cut the line in front of us, I joked with my new friend that no matter how high up you get, there will always be someone ahead of you, so you might as well be happy with your station in life. My new friend shared with me that this is a fundamental principle of Buddhism, and I responded that this is actually a basic tenet of his own faith as well: "*Eizehu ashir hasamei'ach b'chelko*."[171]

> NO MATTER HOW HIGH UP YOU GET, THERE WILL ALWAYS BE SOMEONE AHEAD OF YOU, SO YOU MIGHT AS WELL BE HAPPY WITH YOUR STATION IN LIFE.

---

169    There is a great story of Napoleon scouting out the enemy in a bar and being noticed by the adversary. He allowed his underlings to treat him disrespectfully so that the other side would assume he wasn't really Napoleon. After all, they wouldn't treat the great general so poorly. The man would do whatever necessary to come out on top—even go visit a rabbi!

170    *Vayechi* 49:22.

171    *Avos* 4:1.

This idea was also very emblematic of the message communicated by the tiny menorah of the great Maggid of Kozhnitz—but there wasn't enough time to elaborate just then.

## WHITE HOUSE AMBIENCE

I felt truly small upon entering the White House. Everything is larger than life, ornate and vainglorious. You are greeted by marching bands, soldiers dressed in magnificent colors, and awe-inspiring portraits of former presidents. It was, on some level, the antithesis of the message I had imbibed the previous evening.

In anticipation of this event, I had deliberated what to say to President Obama. Should I say something about Iran or Jonathan Pollard? Or should I stick to domestic issues, such as mental health initiatives and programs for special-needs children? Was saying anything appropriate at all?

IN ANTICIPATION OF THIS EVENT, I HAD DELIBERATED WHAT TO SAY TO PRESIDENT OBAMA.

## SHIFT IN EXPECTATIONS

Upon arriving at the White House, however, I quickly realized that my preparation would be for naught. I would be lucky to shake the President's hand, let alone get in a word or two.[172]

I was reminded of Elisha the prophet offering to speak to the king— meaning the King of kings—on behalf of the Shunamite woman, and her cryptic response that she dwells in the midst of her people.[173] At this party, I, too, would be dwelling in the midst of the masses in attendance, and (unless I would be really rude and aggressive), I would likely not interact with the president at all. Granted, I

I DID FEEL MY HISTORIC MOMENT SLIPPING AWAY.

---

172    I did have a nice conversation with the First Lady. I told her my daughter Anaelle is a big fan and that my daughter believes that she was the real reason that her husband won re-election in 2012. She graciously responded, "You tell your daughter that she is my girl." I had to "look up" to speak with Michelle Obama.

173    *Melachim II* 4:8–37 with the *Zohar* elaborating.

didn't make the choice as the Shunamite did to sit amongst my people and forgo the special access, but I did feel my historic moment slipping away.

Disappointing as it was to discover that I would have no audience with the president, I thought back to the words of the Rebbe the night before and realized that despite all the fanfare, pomp and majesty around me, I was like the little menorah of his ancestor. My most potent influence that afternoon would be in the secluded Red Room of the White House with a small number of my Orthodox brothers, davening the last *Al Hanissim* of Chanukah.

> DESPITE ALL THE FANFARE, POMP AND MAJESTY AROUND ME, I WAS LIKE THE LITTLE MENORAH OF HIS ANCESTOR.

## A SPECIAL TEFILLAH FROM A PLACE OF INFLUENCE

I had special *kavanah* davening in the White House, as the Rebbe had implored me before I left the West Side that morning. He explained that the White House is the place in which decisions affecting Klal Yisrael are made, and to bring *malchus Shamayim* down to such a place by proclaiming *Yehei Shmei Rabbah* there is a tremendous *kiddush Hashem* and could have a profound impact on world events.

I resolved that during the two *tefillos* I would daven in the White House (the last *Minchah* of Chanukah and the first *Maariv* after it), I would focus my additional *Shema Koleinu* requests exclusively on the benefit of Klal Yisrael in Eretz Yisrael. Ultimately, I realized that the influence of the *Yid* is *not* in the halls of power, but rather in the private room of prayer (sealed off by Marine guards) beseeching the "*Malchusa d'Rakia*," the Creator and Mover of all world events.

> THE INFLUENCE OF THE *YID* IS *NOT* IN THE HALLS OF POWER, BUT RATHER IN THE PRIVATE ROOM OF PRAYER.

## DICHOTOMY AND DUALITY

Chazal teach us that a person must always be cognizant of two concepts: *Bishvili nivra ha'olam*—The world was created exclusively for me, and *Anochi afar ve'aifer*—I am but dust and ashes.[174] During this special Chanukah experience I genuinely felt both emotions: honored and privileged to be a representative of our community to the President and First Lady—the *malchusa d'ara*—while simultaneously acknowledging that despite my initial aspirations, I was inconsequential in addressing the most pressing issues of the day, at least vis-à-vis the President. At this critical nexus, I felt comforted by the message of the Maggid of Kozhnitz's little menorah: the message of the power of the *pintele Yid*, the inner fire of the Jew, to search inside himself and seek depth, meaning and connection, and through that internal experience orchestrate events in the highest of realms.

---

174    *Sanhedrin* 37a.

# MY ONE-MINUTE
# SPEECH

give speeches all the time. One could argue that I am a professional speaker. Yet, I was once afforded a speaking opportunity like few others. I was invited by Eric Cantor, the outgoing House Majority Leader, to deliver the opening prayer in the House of Representatives. I would be standing in the exact place that the President of the United States stands each year upon delivering the State of the Union address and where Prime Minister Bibi Netanyahu has now stood three times before a joint session of Congress. I know how to deliver a speech, but a public prayer is something a bit different. I pray daily, but rarely, if ever, verbalize my own personal prayer in public.

## THE SERMON

Congregants often joke about the length of their rabbi's sermon. It isn't really a joke, as more than a few rabbis tend to overstay their welcome on any particular Shabbos morning.[175] Still, even the most time-sensitive congregations tend to give you between five and eight minutes. If you have good stories and jokes, you can stretch it.

This was different. I was given very strict instructions as to content and time limit. I had no more than one hundred and fifty words, which they approximate to be about one minute of speaking time. I had little more than sixty seconds to inspire potentially millions of people and also engage the Speaker of the House and various other lawmakers.[176]

My invitation came immediately after the summer of 2014 discovery of the brutal murder of our three missing boys in Israel, Gilad, Eyal and Naftali, *Hy'd*, as well as the embarrassing revenge attack on an innocent Palestinian boy. Our synagogue was in the forefront of advocating on behalf of the boys

> I HAD LITTLE MORE THAN SIXTY SECONDS TO INSPIRE POTENTIALLY MILLIONS OF PEOPLE AND ALSO ENGAGE THE SPEAKER OF THE HOUSE AND VARIOUS OTHER LAWMAKERS.

through the purchase of a billboard in Times Square.[177] Being honored for our efforts, I was invited to address our House of Representatives.

## CAREFUL SCRUTINY

The text needed to be submitted for approval and I worked hard on what I would say. I wanted to push the envelope a bit and submitted a line that described a "world on fire," including a world where "a mother celebrates her son murdering innocent teenage boys." This was a reference to the mother of one of the kidnappers of the three boys proclaiming she was "proud" if her son was in fact involved in this heinous act. Although, shockingly, a few of our own people committed a similarly dastardly crime, no one celebrated it. In fact, there was mass condemnation—including from the mothers of Gilad, Eyal and Naftali.

Not surprisingly, I received word that the House Chaplain was removing

---

175    There are many good jokes about rabbis speaking too long from the pulpit.
176    C-Span broadcasts live and has millions of viewers.
177    Mentioned earlier in "The Shabbos the Rabbi Dreaded the Sermon."

this line, as it was too provocative and also referenced a foreign policy issue that is against the rules for the daily prayer. This would cost me fifteen words and I badly wanted to maximize my opportunity and get in my fully allotted one hundred and fifty words. I was afraid my audacity would ultimately cost me some precious seconds on my big pulpit.

## LAST-MINUTE EDITS

With a day till the big speech, I quickly revised the line and submitted a new one. I adapted and submitted instead "a world where youthful potential is instantaneously snuffed out without any rhyme or reason." I figured this was broader and captured the sentiments of both sides of the conflict. I was informed this was acceptable, minus the words of "without rhyme or reason," as this too could be controversial or debatable, depending on your world perspective. I was a bit surprised, and also embarrassed to attempt replacing the four words at this late juncture. I would have to live with being a drop short of my allotment.

## SERENDIPITOUS READING

Interestingly, on my way down to Washington, I was reading the biography of the Lubavitcher Rebbe authored by Rabbi Joseph Telushkin. The book has a chapter about the Rebbe's desire and initiative to have Chanukah menorahs lit in the public square.[178] It shares how a certain Reform leader objected to this practice out of fear that this new initiative could raise constitutional establishment clause issues and ultimately create discomfort for our people. I was surprised and gratified to see the Rebbe marshal the prayer I was traveling to give as proof that a mild religious practice, as the menorah, would not in fact offend the Constitution.

I arrived forty-five minutes before "game time" and was invited by Eric Cantor to use his personal office while he attended a briefing IT IS NO SMALL THING TO BE THE ONLY JEWISH REPUBLICAN IN EITHER HOUSE OF CONGRESS AND I WANTED TO THANK HIM FOR HIS STAUNCH REPRESENTATION OF OUR PEOPLE.

---

178    P. 255.

about the Iranian threat. I enjoyed the use of this massive space with its beautiful views overlooking the Capitol and the various historic monuments. Mr. Cantor was a gracious host and I took the opportunity to encourage him and give him *chizuk* over his recent historic primary loss.[179] It is no small thing to be the only Jewish Republican in either House of Congress and I wanted to thank him for his staunch representation of our people. I told him that I was confident he would rebound and accomplish bigger and better things in the near future. He reciprocated by expressing interest in visiting our synagogue on his next trip to New York.

## PHOTO-OPS AND SMALL TALK

There was also an opportunity for a photo-op with Speaker of the House John Boehner. We exchanged some pleasantries about his impressive golf game and my fledgling one, and I thanked him for his staunch support of Israel. In all fairness, I should have presented my name as "David" rather than "Dovid," as the Speaker stumbled on the "o" in my introduction. However, it gave me a good chuckle immediately before going on camera—which was quite helpful in relaxing me.

The experience was exciting and energizing, and I also enjoyed a few other conversations with congressmen from different parts of the country on the House floor. I also spent extra time touring the Capitol with the wonderful members of the House Chaplain's staff. They shared with me that they appreciated my enthusiasm and my being "wide-eyed" about the experience.

## ONE SHINING MOMENT

After some time to reflect, there are some powerful lessons to be gleaned from this unique experience. Firstly, the challenge of formulating something meaningful

IT IS KNOWN IN THE WORLD OF PSYCHOTHERAPY THAT A THERAPIST GENERALLY KEEPS A SESSION TO FORTY-FIVE MINUTES.

---

179    As Mr. Cantor would be leaving office two weeks later, he was particularly relaxed and gracious during my visit.

in just one minute is a daunting one. It is known in the world of psycho-therapy that a therapist generally keeps a session to forty-five minutes. The goal is to focus the patient and be sure they get to the main points quickly. Similarly, I was tasked with formulating something meaningful and getting straight to the point. They even stipulated that no introductory remarks are allowed, and requested that I just go straight into the prayer.

Imagine if everybody had just one minute to make his or her point. Imagine how much time we could all save if things were stripped down to their bare essence. Imagine if your rabbi actually would give a series of one-minute sermons.

Being forced into such an exercise has greatly helped me, especially when formulating longer sermons and speeches.

## QUALITY NOT QUANTITY

Another interesting insight for me was the dearth of people in the House. There were more visiting guests up in the gallery than there were actual representatives in the House. After my prayer, about fifteen representatives awaited their turn to make one-minute pronouncements. I inquired of the congressman next to me as to the point of this. He answered that you take your video clip and disseminate it and show your constituents you are representing them fervently.

I was more shocked when I visited the Senate floor. I learned that passionate speeches made on behalf of Israel by the likes of Ted Cruz, Chuck Schumer and Marco Rubio were likely

THERE WAS LIKELY LESS THAN A *MINYAN* (OR MAYBE EVEN A *MEZUMAN*) IN ATTENDANCE AT THOSE PRESENTATIONS.

not stated in front of masses of people. There was likely less than a *minyan* (or maybe even a *mezuman*) in attendance at those presentations.

However, they understand their backdrop and forum is a means to an end. It is a powerful place from which to project a message that then can be shared with the world. I too, have come to appreciate how an article written in the confines of my office or a speech given to a small crowd still has the power (in our technologically sophisticated age) to travel very far and wide. I was comforted in knowing that even our lawmakers don't always speak in front of the biggest crowds. It reinforced for me not to get bogged down in the surrounding details but rather focus on the core message, as they do.

## A COUNTRY OF KINDNESS

It was really something extraordinary to stand and speak in our nation's capitol. It affirmed for me the greatness of our country and the religious freedom and tolerance that we so richly benefit from. That I can speak freely with those who shape our laws is not something that I take lightly or for granted.

## LIFE LESSONS

The lessons I learned were more far-reaching as well. I view time very differently these days.

Who among us wasn't shattered when we read about the losses of young Israeli soldiers in various wars to protect our homeland—whose lives are snuffed out in one brief moment?

How do we fill our time? Use our minutes?

Our clocks are ticking and every moment counts. As Rabbi Yosef Dov Soloveitchik so poignantly put it: "We play our parts and then quickly get off the stage."[180] As the fickleness and uncertainty of life plays out before our very eyes each day, it behooves us to fill up our minutes—to adopt the mantra of "carpe diem."

> WE PLAY OUR PARTS AND THEN QUICKLY GET OFF THE STAGE.

## MITZVAH PREGAME

Rabbi Wolbe suggests that a person should dedicate at least a minute

---

180    The Rav echoing the great poet William Shakespeare.

a day to prepare for davening.[181] Just as *chassidim ha-rishonim* prepared for *tefillah*,[182] we too shouldn't rush into shul just in time.

When I first heard this, years ago, I was surprised that he suggested such a brief period of time. After my experience at the House of Repre-sentatives, I began to understand what a person can invest in one minute. Perhaps Rabbi Wolbe was suggesting that a given period of time, albeit concise, but invested

> AFTER MY EXPERIENCE AT THE HOUSE OF REPRESENTATIVES, I BEGAN TO UNDERSTAND WHAT A PERSON CAN INVEST IN ONE MINUTE.

with framing, orienting and determining a core approach to that day's prayers, can go a long way.

In secular society, there is something called a "moment of silence," during which observers silently reflect, remember and show respect. It is also a time to say in silence what can't be said in words. Let us take a moment—one minute—to truly appreciate the *brachah* of just one more minute, and to dedicate it to our Creator and His people, with all the spiritual energy and focus we can muster.

To be truly alive, for just one moment in time!

---

181    "Vaadim on Tefillah" from *Alei Shur, chelek beis*, begins on p. 348.
182    *Berachos* 30b.

# MUSINGS ON AFFLUENCE AND CHARITABLE GIVING

recently noticed, while being present and attentive at my Shabbos table, that much of the conversation was focused on money. My guests were just enamored with the bank accounts of others. I found myself perplexed as to how this became the main topic of conversation at the table week after week.

I have lived predominantly in two locales in my lifetime. Five years in Israel, predominantly in Jerusalem, and the rest in the New York metropolitan area, the most recent nine on the Upper West Side of Manhattan. From my limited vantage point, two very distinct currencies are at play.

## PRIMACY OF SPIRITUAL VALUES

In Jerusalem, the currency of primary value, that which gives you the most honor or respect in the eyes of others, is the amount of Torah you have amassed. I had the great privilege of living in Har Nof and marveled at the levels of scholarship that walked the streets, whether it was Rabbi Ovadia Yosef, Rabbi Moshe Sternbuch, Rabbi Shlomo Fischer, Rabbi Ariev Ozer, just to name a few. A person of stature in learning on the Upper West Side of Manhattan could be a total ignoramus on the streets of Har Nof.

Ironically, it is interesting that the neighborhood of Rabbi Shlomo Zalman Auerbach, Shaarei Chesed/Rechavia, once a very humble locale, has seen an explosion of multi-million dollar homes in the last fifteen years or so. The little domain of this great *gadol* has been rebuilt into a fortress.[183] There is great Torah (his son Rabbi Shmuel Auerbach for example) enmeshed together with great affluence in this community.

## MATERIAL PROWESS AND PROSPERITY

In America, and particularly in parts of New York and Los Angeles, the emphasis seems to be more on net financial worth. The more money you have, the more impressive, awe-inspiring and deserving of *kavod* and reverence. People are impressed by money. Money buys power, influence and a certain amount of control. It used to be that being a millionaire was really something. Nowadays the numbers have gotten significantly larger.

IT USED TO BE THAT BEING A MILLIONAIRE WAS REALLY SOMETHING.

There are Orthodox Jews that possess hundreds of millions if not billions of dollars. Generational wealth is becoming more common in our communities due to tremendous success in finance and real estate. There

---

183    One of the highlights of my early yeshiva years in Israel post high school was escorting the *Gadol Ha-dor* walking from the Gra shul to his small and modest home up the hill. We locked arms and discussed methodologies of Torah study and the *bircas kohanim* that he stressed must be given over with love. I recall the conversation like it was yesterday.

are Orthodox Jews who own stakes in professional sports teams and Orthodox Jews who have private jets and multiple award-winning homes along with various other unimaginable luxuries. I actually have even met some of these people.

## OH, THAT WARM FUZZY FEELING

There is something intoxicating about being in the presence of such people. As if somehow some of the magic touch can rub off on others. *Lehavdil*, just like for some people it can feel amazing to be in the presence of Rabbi Chaim Kanievsky or other *gedolei Yisrael*, for others, association with extremely wealthy people also brings some palpable, albeit ephemeral, euphoria. Amazingly, sometimes the same people are uplifted by both experiences.

I recall listening to Aaron Wolfson eulogize his father, the renowned philanthropist, Zev Wolfson. He commented that his father taught him that no matter how important or wealthy the person they were meeting was, that person put on a pair of pants in the morning the same way that they did. It was ironic to listen to a very rich man teach everybody else how to deal with people like himself—the message being that ultimately we are all human beings at the end of the day. Being wealthy is surely a *brachah* and I'm sure at times even a challenge, but ultimately it is just a description and not definitional of whom the person really is at the core.

HIS FATHER TAUGHT HIM THAT NO MATTER HOW IMPORTANT OR WEALTHY THE PERSON THEY WERE MEETING WAS, THAT PERSON PUT ON A PAIR OF PANTS IN THE MORNING THE SAME WAY THAT THEY DID.

## WHAT YOU PRAISE AND EAT

The verse in *Mishlei*[184] famously comments, "*Ish l'fi mehalelo*," that a person is evaluated by his praise.[185] This is explained to mean that we can

---

184　27:21.
185　Rabbi Hutner discussed this concept in his opening salvo of his *Pachad Yitzchak* on Purim.

discern much about a person's aspirations in life by what they admire and talk about. Do they emphasize spirituality and growth-oriented people or do they spend their time admiring the physical beauty and possessions of others? This is the Jewish manifestation or incarnation of "you are what you eat."[186]

Wealth can be intoxicating, but we must be sure that we aren't blinded. Most would choose it if it came their way, because it helps in many realms of life, but why is it deserving of so much respect and discussion? Maybe if a person overcomes the challenge of affluence and is still of exemplary character and down-to-earth despite inordinate wealth, it is worthy of mention, but beyond that, why do many fixate on it so much? For those who don't possess great wealth but are still so enamored with it, perhaps reflecting on this disconnect is called for. What is really gained from the gawking?

## SHOW ME THE MONEY

On the flip side, affluence brings on many charitable requests for *tzedakah* as well as heavy communal expectations. Some wealthy people enjoy this role more than others. Some delegate the distributions to a *gabbai* while others handle the requests themselves. Some affluent people really attempt to keep a

SOME AFFLUENT PEOPLE REALLY ATTEMPT TO KEEP A LOW PROFILE WHILE OTHERS ARE HAPPY TO HAVE THEIR BLESSINGS AND BOUNTY ACKNOWLEDGED PUBLICLY.

---

186    This phrase has come to us via quite a tortuous route. In *Physiologie du Gout, ou Meditations de Gastronomie Transcendante (1826)*, Anthelme Brillat-Savarin wrote: "*Dis-moi ce que tu manges, je te dirai ce que tu es.*" (Tell me what you eat and I will tell you what you are.) In an essay titled Concerning Spiritualism and Materialism, 1863/4, Ludwig Andreas Feuerbach wrote: "*Der Mensch ist, was er ißt.*" That translates into English as "man is what he eats." Neither Brillat-Savarin or Feuerbach meant for their quotations to be taken literally. They were stating that the food one eats has a bearing on one's state of mind and health. The actual phrase didn't emerge in English until sometime later. In the 1920s and 30s, the nutritionist Victor Lindlahr, who was a strong believer in the idea that food controls health, developed the Catabolic Diet. That view gained some adherents at the time and the earliest known printed example is from an advert for beef in a 1923 edition of the *Bridgeport Telegraph*, for United Meet [sic] Markets: "Ninety percent of the diseases known to man are caused by cheap foodstuffs. You are what you eat."

low profile while others are happy to have their blessings and bounty acknowledged publicly. Each has unique reasons and systems for distribution and attitude.

Many such people approach *tzedakah* or charitable giving the way they approach business. They see it as an investment and they'd like to be confident in the return on investment, or ROI. Others are insistent on the form of the solicitation, meaning that a significant sum must be requested face-to-face and not hiding behind an email or letter, despite the difficulty in arranging such a meeting.

## THE WEALTHIER THE BIGGER THE DONATION? THINK AGAIN!

People often assume that the more one has quantitatively, the more you can get from them, but it is often the opposite. The more sophisticated the donor in financial matters and the more successful, the harder it will be to convince them to invest in your cause. Most of them became wealthy for a reason—with an eye toward discerning a good investment from a bad one.

## REPETITIVE ACTION AND INDOCTRINATION

We say in the third blessing of the *bentching*, or Grace after Meals, that we desire sustenance through His full and open hands and not from human beings. Though some people have a high embarrassment quotient for asking for charity, it is ultimately a terrible feeling to have to ask anybody for money or financial help.

The Rambam says that it is preferable to give out a hundred one-dollar bills over just one hundred-dollar bill so that we cultivate a giving spirit.[187] Everybody should give something, even when we frown on the cause. If Hashem blessed someone with tremendous wealth, that token giving should be a respectable number for a person of such means. This

---

187    Commentary to *Avos* 3:15.

is ultimately how we refine our *middos*, which may be why Hashem has blessed us with affluence.

## SPEAK SOFTLY AND CARRY A SMALL STICK

Finally, if someone just can't give, because they view charitable giving like investing or because they are just put off by the request, please don't judge or begrudge the person who asks. Try to be compassionate when turning a person down. Let them know that you appreciate their difficult situation and wish you could help but you just can't right now. There is no need to add insult to injury by implying in any way that you look down upon the person asking or that you feel they need to be doing more for themselves. They likely feel low enough already and if they don't, I'm not sure it is your responsibility to change their attitude.

THERE IS NO NEED TO ADD INSULT TO INJURY BY IMPLYING IN ANY WAY THAT YOU LOOK DOWN UPON THE PERSON ASKING OR THAT YOU FEEL THEY NEED TO BE DOING MORE FOR THEMSELVES.

There is an ever-growing disconnect in our communities between people of different levels of resources. It impacts communal social interactions with the affluent becoming more secluded and private and others feeling shunned, hurt and sometimes just not good enough.[188]

More thought has to be given to bridging this developing chasm and more introspection on both sides of the divide in terms of how each is perceived and the subtle messages that are being sent. May Hashem bless each of us with what we need and with the ultimate wealth as defined by our ancestors in *Pirkei Avos*—being truly content with our lots in life![189]

---

188     I recall, early in my career, a woman coming to my office and crying about how her family felt completely shunned socially because she was on a different and lower financial track then her neighbors.

189     *Avos* 3:1.

# SECTION SIX

## Strengthening Faith in Our Turbulent Times

# YEARNING FOR A CANDY MAN

n reading the story of the Jewish people crossing the sea, I find it striking that the women, led by Miriam, sing their own song. In fact, they have various musical instruments and seemingly are outdoing the men.

Is this activity motivated by some feminist agenda?

Or could it be an expression of modesty, as displayed in an Orthodox synagogue?

> Miriam the prophetess, the sister of Aaron, took the tambourine in her hand and all the women went forth after her with tambourines and with dances.[190]

An interesting suggestion is that the Torah is describing Miriam as a prophetess and as the sister of Aharon before embarking on her unique

---

190    *Beshalach* 15:20.

song of praise. Chazal inform us that Miriam revealed to her parents that they would have a son who would redeem the Jewish people from Egypt.[191] Due to her prophecy, her parents were motivated to reunite. Thus, Moshe was conceived, despite the ominous decree leveled against male babies in Egypt.

## SUSPENSE AND INTRIGUE

The challenge or tension of the story is watching Moshe develop into a leader while avoiding the proverbial target on his back. It echoes the tension that we often have when reading tense stories in the Torah, such as the story of Yosef and his brothers.[192] Although we know the conclusion of the various anecdotes from year to year, we still anxiously read the stories as they unfold and feel the fear, concern or excitement as if events are happening in real time. Similarly, we know Moshe comes out successfully, but as we trace the story from its origins, that conclusion seems far from assured or secure.

> ALTHOUGH WE KNOW THE CONCLUSION OF THE VARIOUS ANECDOTES FROM YEAR TO YEAR, WE STILL ANXIOUSLY READ THE STORIES AS THEY UNFOLD AND FEEL THE FEAR, CONCERN OR EXCITEMENT AS IF EVENTS ARE HAPPENING IN REAL TIME.

## UNWAVERING FAITH

Miriam watches from the sidelines as baby Moshe is floating in a basket on the sea. Along comes the daughter of the man who decreed that Moshe should be killed. The situation looks dire. Yet, Miriam believes Hashem will come through. Despite what she sees before her eyes, in the recesses of her heart she knows differently. Sure enough, the daughter of the Egyptian ruler ultimately spares the child.

Years later, there is similar language when our people are locked in at sea, trapped between the water and the Egyptians.

---

191    *Sotah* 11b.
192    Yosef reveals himself at the beginning of *Vayigash* (44:18).

> Moses said to the people, "Do not fear! Stand fast and see the sal-
> vation of Hashem that He will perform for you today; for that which
> you have seen Egypt today, you shall not see them ever again![193]

Moshe—the same Moshe who was pulled from the water and saved as
a baby—tells his people not to fear. He tells them to stand firm and watch
the salvation Hashem will bring them.

He is really telling them, "Sit back like my sister Miriam did and watch
what Hashem will do. You think the situation is hopeless, but you will see
otherwise."

## THE EPIPHANY

This sheds light on Miriam singing an additional song by the Splitting
of the Sea. At this moment, as the Jews are redeemed from Egypt, she
experiences the culmination of her personal prophecy of years ago. This
is why the verse leading into the song accents her being a prophetess as
well as the sister of Aharon. It brings us full circle and is a celebration of
the culmination of years of aspiring and hoping for the development of
baby Moshe into the Moshe Rabbeinu Hashem promised.

One of the great challenges in *emunah* today is not so much believing
that Hashem can fix all problems but rather accepting that if the situation has not yet been "fixed," it is because He has chosen not to address
it in the way we would have hoped. Not every story has a happy ending,
at least in this world.

Klal Yisrael as a nation has a promise or prophecy of redemption[194]—
but no individual necessarily does.

## MATURATION IN RELATING TO G-D

In my work as a congregational rabbi, I have observed a certain phenomenon over the years. When people are suffering a personal difficulty

---

193    *Beshalach* 14:13.
194    *Yirmiyahu* 31:14.

or disappointment, they will often question G-d. Where is G-d? What happened to G-d?[195] Often, they begin to say it isn't worth serving G-d if He won't come through for me when I need Him most. I refer to this phenomenon as "G-d as candy man."

Sadly, people have a childish image of "the man upstairs" as there primarily to perform their bidding.

> SADLY, PEOPLE HAVE A CHILDISH IMAGE OF "THE MAN UPSTAIRS" AS THERE PRIMARILY TO PERFORM THEIR BIDDING.

It isn't easy to sublimate our wishes to a higher will, to introspect and understand that there is a purpose to suffering, trial and tribulation and that we are being guided and held by the ultimate Being in our greatest times of need. The purpose of all events is to deepen our relationship and faith in G-d. To do this, we need to mature in our view of G-d—to believe that only He really knows what is best for us and that it is completely possible that we can't appreciate or understand His will. Some of us are stronger in this worldview than others.[196]

> THE PURPOSE OF ALL EVENTS IS TO DEEPEN OUR RELATIONSHIP AND FAITH IN G-D.

The question of faith has gnawed at us throughout Jewish history. Questions about why the righteous suffer and the evil thrive have been addressed for generations.[197] History is rife with questions and not always filled with adequate answers.[198] One day we will understand the

---

195    It amazes me how often people have a crisis of faith. It is usually when something is going wrong. I have never had a person come with a crisis of faith when life was going the way they had hoped it would!

196    When communicating this concept, I often think of the time one of my kids was getting stitches and the plastic surgeon requested that I hold my child down. My son wanted to kill me and was livid at me for doing this. However, this pain that I was contributing to was in reality a great benefit for him as I was facilitating the healing process. My son had no comprehension in the moment what a kindness I was performing for him, but in reality, with a closer look, this was exactly what I was doing. Many times in life, Hashem acts like the parent who holds down the child. The process is painful for Hashem, as it was for me when I was instructed to hold down my son, but ultimately the parent does what he knows is best for the child, and the parents can see the bigger picture that the child often misses.

197    Rabbi Eliyahu Dessler in his *Michtav Me'eliyahu* has a cogent essay and analysis of this intricate topic, along with many other great Jewish philosphers.

198    To quote Rebbetzin Basha Twersky, the wife of the murdered Rabbi Moshe Twersky, *Hy"d* in the Har Nof shul in November 2014, "If we have any questions, it is the same questions that

entire progression of world history and our people's unique placement within it. For now we need adequate patience until the final redemption with the arrival of Mashiach. Until then we must continue to hold on tight and trust that there will one day be a happy communal ending.

## WHAT CAN YOU DO?

We can't sit back like Miriam does by the water or as the nation does years later by the Splitting of the Sea. They didn't know *how* Hashem would come through for them, but they had a commitment that He *would*.

We, as individuals, can't be comforted in this way. We have no "guarantee" that things will work out. What can we do?

> WE HAVE NO "GUARANTEE" THAT THINGS WILL WORK OUT. WHAT CAN WE DO?

We need to trust, and act. Trust G-d, but care for each other. Trust G-d, but do extra *mitzvos*. Trust G-d, but reach out and show concern for Jews who are different than we are—and ones we may even disagree with.

Our trump card, then, is to pivot and redouble our efforts to connect with Klal Yisrael. The more we are connected to other Jews, the more connected we are to national salvation. This is because ultimately it is only the community that is promised the happy ending. If we unite and join Klal Yisrael through our actions, deeds and thoughts, we

> IF WE UNITE AND JOIN KLAL YISRAEL THROUGH OUR ACTIONS, DEEDS AND THOUGHTS, WE POSITION OURSELVES TO REJOICE IN THE FINAL REDEMPTION.

position ourselves to rejoice in the final redemption. As Chazal teach us, whoever cries over the destruction of the Temple and joins in the communal mourning, will ultimately rejoice in the rebuilding of that same structure.[199]

---

Jews have been asking for thousands of years."

199    *Bava Basra* 60b.

# IN EVERY
# GENERATION

**W**hen I think of people dying *al kiddush Hashem*[200] (sanctification of G-d's name) and *mesiras nefesh* (self-sacrifice), I tend to focus on the Holocaust or earlier generations in our history. Our generation, with its material comforts and affluence, doesn't initially come to mind. I therefore was perplexed and surprised when reflecting on (just some of) the Jews killed in recent years simply due to the fact that they were Jews: the eight boys learning in Mercaz Ha-Rav; the five members of the Fogel family (including a three-month-old baby girl) in Itamar; the Holtzbergs (Chabad *shluchim* in Mumbai, India); Baruch Sandler and his two children in Toulouse, France; the triple murder of Eyal Yifrach, Naftali Fraenkel and Gilad Shaar; the five victims of the Har Nof massacre, and additional shocking non-random murders of Jews in European cities in groceries and shuls.

---

200    Dying to defend the faith or being targeted specifically because one is a Jew.

Unfortunately, many others, including all the victims of Arab terror, could and should be on this list.

Furthermore, there are countless others who have been attacked by anti-Semites and murderers. It seems as if we aren't living in as safe of a generation as is commonly thought.

## ALWAYS A TARGET

I guess I shouldn't be surprised. We say in the Passover Haggadah, "In every generation they stand up against us to destroy us."[201] In truth, to many in our generation those were always just words. But when considering the stockpiled evidence, we have no choice but to acknowledge that it speaks to our generation as well. The vulnerability we all feel is acute and real.

"IN EVERY GENERATION THEY STAND UP AGAINST US TO DESTROY US." WHEN CONSIDERING THE EVIDENCE, IT IS CLEAR THAT THIS SPEAKS TO OUR GENERATION AS WELL.

We've heard countless stories of inspiring visits to the various shivah homes of these tragedies. One rabbi who visited from America[202] reported that on the gate entering the Fraenkel home the following words were written: *"Am ha-netzach eino mefached mi-derech arukah"*[203]—An eternal people doesn't fear the long journey. He said the words spoke much louder than any long sermon he could possibly give.

AN ETERNAL PEOPLE DOESN'T FEAR THE LONG JOURNEY.

These poignant and powerful words moved me to tears. They represent to me our total trust in Hashem that we will ultimately be redeemed, though we understand that there will be great difficulties and sacrifices along the way.

My tears flowed from the realization that those on the front lines of the suffering have understood and embraced this reality wholeheartedly. Frankly, I had never seen anything quite like it in my life.

---

201    In the early part of the *Maggid* section of the Haggadah. Immediately after, we explicate what Lavan Haarami did to Yaakov Aveinu.

202    Rabbi Tzvi Hersh Weinreb of the OU.

203    Writings of Rabbi Kook.

## THE TALKING DONKEY

We read in *Parshas Balak* how Hashem opens up the mouth of the donkey. The donkey asks Bilam what it did to deserve being hit three "times."[204]

The anomaly is that rather than using the word "*pe'amim*" (times), the Torah uses "*regalim*," the word we traditionally use to describe our three Festivals. Rashi tells us the Torah is alluding to Bilam's desire to eradicate a people—those who celebrate the three Festivals of the year.

The Maharal of Prague in *Gur Aryeh*, his commentary on Rashi, elucidates this by explaining the uniqueness of the three Festivals and why the donkey focuses on that particular mitzvah. He explains that time is comprised of past, present and future—and the message of the donkey is that our people have prevailed through past and present and will survive into the future. Hashem gives us the three Festivals to inculcate within us our dominion over (and permanence within) time.

> THE MESSAGE OF THE DONKEY IS THAT OUR PEOPLE HAVE PREVAILED THROUGH PAST AND PRESENT AND WILL SURVIVE INTO THE FUTURE.

## THE SEASONS AND THE FESTIVALS

All three Festivals are situated within the warmer months, filled with hope and light, in contrast to the winter months, which represent death and stagnation. The donkey is rebuking and challenging Bilam over his desire to harm a nation that rejoices within the times of growth and potential. This joy embedded within the growth season reflects our eternality, timelessness, completeness and yearning for ultimate tranquility.

> THE JOY EMBEDDED WITHIN THE GROWTH SEASON REFLECTS OUR ETERNALITY, TIMELESSNESS, COMPLETENESS AND YEARNING FOR ULTIMATE TRANQUILITY.

Bilam, representing the archetype of our enemies throughout the centuries, is rebuffed by the symbolism of an eternal people, accented and

---

highlighted by the placement of our three Festivals—an eternal people not afraid of the long and difficult road home.

## US VS. THEM

In the fifth chapter of *Avos*, we are taught the contrasting natures of the students of Avraham and the students of Bilam.[205] The qualities of Avraham's descendants are a good eye and a humble spirit in physical and spiritual pursuits. Mrs. Racheli Fraenkel, as well as the other two heroic mothers of the three teenagers, displayed these qualities repeatedly throughout eighteen days of uncertainty. Constantly acknowledging and thanking people from all walks of Jewish life, seeing only the good, they were and are the quintessential bearers of the legacy of Avraham Avinu.

The remarks of Mrs. Fraenkel to young women at the Kotel were a beautiful manifestation of that legacy. To insist that "Hashem doesn't work for us" and that we can't lose faith even with a negative outcome was awe-inspiring—even more so when it became clear (after the fact) that she was bracing the nation for the blow she felt was likely coming.

Let us not lose sight of what we are here to accomplish, of our mission to bring honor to our Creator in whatever situation He challenges us with. Our frustration,

> TO INSIST THAT "HASHEM DOESN'T WORK FOR US" AND THAT WE CAN'T LOSE FAITH EVEN WITH A NEGATIVE OUTCOME WAS AWE-INSPIRING.

sadness and even anger cannot lead to impetuousness or foolishness. We are the eternal people and as such should not fear the long road home.

---

205    *Avos* 5:19.

# HURRICANE SEASON

t's been a rough few weeks.

It began with the news of a heinous crime just blocks from where I live on Manhattan's Upper West Side: a nanny viciously took the lives of her two young charges.

Hurricane Sandy came next, contributing additional loss of life and financial devastation, of a magnitude never before experienced in these parts.

A week later, many in our community were disappointed with the decisive outcome of the presidential election and the realization that we are truly a minority both in number and outlook within the United States. (My young daughter informed me she voted in her mock school election for Mitt Romney. Why? She said he'd be a good friend to Israel and "lower the price of taxis."[206])

> SHE SAID HE'D BE A GOOD FRIEND TO ISRAEL AND "LOWER THE PRICE OF TAXIS."

Finally, there was the precarious situation in Eretz Yisrael—hundreds of rockets raining down daily and the threat of another major war.

---

206    She intended to say "taxes"!

As the saying goes, "When it rains, it pours."

To lend insight to these complicated developments and events, a look at the beginning of the Torah and certain key personalities is helpful.

## A BRILLIANT PATRIARCHAL TRILOGY

The Book of Bereishis focuses on the *Avos*. In Kabbalistic writings, Avraham Avinu is an archetype, representing and epitomizing G-d's trait of *chesed*, or kindness.[207] This symbolism of Divine kindness, represented in the persona of Avraham, is palpable all the time, but most sharply in the first month of the Jewish calendar. Tishrei is all kindness from Hashem, His accepting our *teshuvah*, cleansing us and allowing us to sit in the *sukkah* under His watchful eye.

Bereishis then shifts to the stories of Yitzchak Avinu and the aspects of judgment or intensity of his persona as exemplified in the Akeidah experience. The letters of "Yitzchak" spell "*ketz hai*," meaning end of life, as he represents the transition into a higher world and the finality and magnitude of death. Yitzchak is also an archetype, representing difficulty—fitting for the recent times of disappointment, anguish and pain. He is also connected to the period of Shavuos and the intensity of our receiving the Torah with a mountain held over our heads.

Finally, there is the persona of the grandson Yaakov Avinu. He represents to us a progression and development, integrating Divine traits exhibited by his holy ancestors. In difficult times alluded to above, his efforts at integration are emblematic of what we seek from Hashem—that He be inspired by Yaakov's trait of *tiferes*; that Hashem look toward the integration, balance and synthesis Yaakov created and use it as a model of tempering His strict justice, *din*, with Divine mercy, *rachamim*. Just as Yaakov integrated the *chesed* of his grandfather and the *din* of his father, we pray that Hashem will also integrate mercy within His judgment.[208]

---

207  Adapted from a wonderful *shiur* I heard many years ago from Rabbi Michael Rosensweig, a Rosh Yeshiva and Rosh Kollel at Yeshivat Rabeinu Yitzchok Elchonon in NYC.

208  This echoes the concept of Hashem tempering the creation of the world with His kindness, as the world wouldn't last with just strict judgment. The development and fine-tuning of the traits of the Patriarchs, possibly echoes the traits Hashem used in the creation of the world

This is expressed in the festival of Sukkos juxtaposed with the judgment of Rosh Hashanah/Yom Kippur but now expressing the joy of being under the temporal hut reflecting faith and Divine protection.[209]

## THE AGE OF ANXIETY

Even before the recent difficult events, we live in an age of anxiety. Many of us strive for an equanimity or psychological stability in our lives. This goal has been made most difficult to achieve by the ongoing economic ills and the general challenges of living in the technological age.

There is a quiet tension that lurks inside many of us: If I have *emunah*, why all the anxiety?

IF I HAVE *EMUNAH*, WHY ALL THE ANXIETY?

In a sense, that's like asking, if I have *yiras Shamayim*, why do I ever sin?[210]

We all have lapses, but we add to our stress levels when we are self-critical, thinking that we aren't authentic or genuine in our *avodah*. We often forget that many great people have had these common setbacks and challenges.

## SARAH'S YEARS

The Reszher Rebbe, Rabbi Aaron Levine, commented on the life of Sarah being one hundred and twenty-seven years and the fact that her years were, as Chazal teach, "all equally for the good."[211] He suggests that she was a model for balanced, emotionally healthy living. She remained even-keeled despite numerous challenges: On the one hand, she is uprooted from her homeland and abducted by a foreign king. Yet, she also experiences great affluence and is the recipient of an enormous and miraculous

---

and they are possibly a reflection or mirror for us to remind Hashem through our *zechus avos* to go a little easier on us.

209   Tur links the three Avos to the three Festivals.

210   Rabbi Wolbe discusses such a query in *Alei Shur, chelek beis*. Perfect *yiras Shamayim* theoretically would preclude sin.

211   Rashi on beginning of *Chayei Sarah*, where the *pasuk* spells out by bifurcating the one hundred and twenty-seven years of her life.

Divine gift with the birth of Yitzchak. Amazingly, her basic decency and humanity isn't impacted by either course of events. As Rudyard Kipling famously wrote in his poem "If," she "walks with kings without losing the common touch." All her one hundred and twenty-seven years were "equally for the good."

## OF WEDDINGS AND FUNERALS

Equilibrium is echoed by the sevens of *sheva berachos* and *sheva yemei aveilus* and also the juxtaposition of the burial of Sarah and the finding of a wife for Yitzchak. A wholesome spiritual life will have ups and downs.[212] At the wedding, the pinnacle of joy, we reflect on the Churban, the destruction of the Temple. In mourning, we have limitations

A GREAT CHALLENGE OF LIFE IS STAYING IN SYNC AND NOT BENDING OUT OF SORTS OR TO EXTREMES.

that don't expand beyond a year. We balance and temper all emotions because when we are out of sorts, we can't serve the Divine in the requisite inspired fashion. A great challenge of life is staying in sync and not bending out of sorts or to extremes.[213]

A mentor of mine once said, *"Ha-chaim zeh lo piknik,"*[214] which translates to, "Life isn't easy." I was on the Upper West Side of Manhattan during Hurricane Sandy. We didn't lose electricity. In fact, we barely felt a thing. This was not the case for our neighbors in many other places. Everyone goes through struggles. Some are more readily visible while others are more latent, but we all have stress, as this world is one of tests.

## REALLY LISTENING TO OTHERS

How can I connect to other people's difficulties? Connection for me comes when I reflect on the birth of my oldest child, who—as a complete shock to us at the time—entered our world with a diagnosis of Down

---

212    They say in Arabic, *"yom asal, yom basal,"* a day of onion and a day of honey.
213    Rambam, *Hilchos Deos*, *perek* 1, *shvil ha-zahav* or "golden mean."
214    Rabbi Ari Waxman of Sha'alvim, mentioned in earlier pieces.

syndrome. Those first few days were incredibly difficult. All thoughts of the future were frightening and overwhelming. The challenge for us was to stay afloat and regain equilibrium. We all go through this in different ways, at different times.

In the hard times, it is crucial that we share our feelings and express ourselves. It's healthy to acknowledge the fear and doubts and to lean on others for support. Chazal teach: "*Daagah b'lev ish yasichenu l'acher*—Worry in the heart of man should be expressed to others."[215] We need to listen to others—and we need people to listen to us, whether listening professionals or good friends and family.[216]

**WE NEED TO LISTEN TO OTHERS–AND WE NEED PEOPLE TO LISTEN TO US.**

## YAAKOV AND YISRAEL

Yaakov introduced *Maariv*, the evening prayer.[217] In the darkness of night, when there is a tremendous lack of clarity, Yaakov, who represents us, Bnei Yisrael, cries out to Hashem. Hashem is the address we can always turn to no matter how dark the darkness and despair. The synthesizing of *chesed* with *din*, the enmeshing of these two phenomena emanate from our father Yaakov, who prayed from the darkness.

Even so, one must remember the maxim introduced by Rabbi Yitzchak Hutner in a famous letter to a struggling student, "Lose the battle, but win the war."[218] We have lost some battles of late, but we must always keep our "eye on the prize" and fight to the finish, where a splendorous redemption awaits us just beyond the horizon.

**LOSE THE BATTLE, BUT WIN THE WAR.**

---

215    *Yoma* 75a.

216    I heard of a very successful mental health professional who is asked, "How do you listen to people's problems all day?" His answer is, "Who's listening?" I think that beneath the humor, he is expressing the reality of much of what he does. We are so inundated with our own personal "stuff" that it is hard to be there for someone else.

217    *Berachos* 26b.

218    *Pachad Yitzchak, Iggros U'ketavim* #128 (referenced earlier).

# BEHEADING ISIS

onservative columnist for the *Boston Globe* Jeff Jacoby explains that the Islamic State (ISIS) has used the traumatic and dramatic tactic of beheading to strike fear and terror in their adversaries' hearts as they attempt to conquer Iraq and Syria.[219] He mentions the painful examples of journalists and relief workers James Foley, Steven Sotloff and David Haines as indicative of the psychological warfare being implemented. Significantly, and contrary to comments of President Obama, he adds that beheading is also part of Muslim theology and history. The Koran explicitly states, "When you meet the unbelievers, smite their necks."[220] He explains that this verse is interpreted by leading Islamic scholars as a directive to literally behead such individuals.

## MIND/BODY CONNECTION

It is interesting to me that, *lehavdil*, the High Holiday of Rosh Hashanah

---

219     *Boston Globe* 9/22/14.
220     *Sura* 8:12.

accents the beginning, the *rosh*, or "head of the new year." Jewish esoteric sources comment that the three core Festivals of Pesach, Shavuos and Sukkos are parallel to the inherent traits of the three Patriarchs and represent different aspects or parts of the human body.[221]

In contrast, Rosh Hashanah represents the head. The relationship between Rosh Hashanah and the other three Festivals is comparable to the relationship between the head and the other body parts. Rabbi Shimshon Pincus explains this further and suggests that arms, legs, eyes and ears all have a certain limited expanse or range they can reach. They each capture a limited terrain in the realm of space. In parallel, the mind and its imaginative capacity are able to traverse time and reach all the way to the higher spheres of the heavens.

## UNLIMITED POTENTIAL

The core message then of the Jewish New Year is our limitless potential and capacity. The day is an expression of the limitless perception of the mind. This potential is apparent on the day that celebrates the anniversary of the creation of man. On that initial day, original man was created perfectly with an incredible breadth and length of being, both in spiritual and physical talent and reach. Strikingly, the Brisker Rav noted that in the initial week after birth, a person's purest natural tendencies and predilections are most discernible. After that, he argues, the baby begins to imitate and continues on this path for the rest of its life.

THE CORE MESSAGE THEN OF THE JEWISH NEW YEAR IS OUR LIMITLESS POTENTIAL AND CAPACITY.

Generally, we assume G-d has the amazing ability to create something from nothing (*yesh me'ayin*) while we only have the ability to create something from something (*yesh me'yesh*). Yet, on Rosh Hashanah, we too have the ability to dream and to imagine new horizons and the creation of (seemingly) something from nothing.

Rabbi Pincus brings an interesting parable. Although we have many

---

221   Most of the Torah in this piece is rooted in an essay by Rabbi Shimshon Pincus in the *sefer* of his lectures on Yomim Noraim/Rosh Hashanah, p. 329.

personal aspirations and requests during this period, nobody prays for a third eye. This is presumably due to the reality that nobody believes it possible. In truth, a third eye could be very handy, yet nobody wastes time praying for such a thing. Yet our matriarch Sarah conceived a much-desired child on Rosh Hashanah, even though our rabbis teach that she lacked a uterus and thus the capacity to carry a child. Embedded within this initial day of the year is a miraculous, almost supernatural, *yesh me'ayin* capacity for growth waiting to be accessed.

## ISIS AND AMALEK

One can posit that ISIS is a current-day manifestation of Amalek, our historical archenemy, per the insight of Rabbi Chaim Brisker in understanding a Rambam.[222] The etymology of Amalek stems from the Torah word "*melikah*," the process of snapping the neck of a bird as atonement for our sins. Its imagery communicates that our being stiff-necked resulted in our pursuing a direction opposite from G-d. This process and mechanism of our sacrificing a bird is a realization that inflexibility harms spiritual growth. We *do* possess the ability to change and seek a different road. The symbolism of this sacrificial process is the lesson that a head turns upon the body and can see new vistas and perspectives, an allusion to the authentic aim of Rosh Hashanah, which is change, growth and movement.

ONE CAN POSIT THAT ISIS IS A CURRENT DAY MANIFESTATION OF AMALEK, OUR HISTORICAL ARCHENEMY.

ISIS beheads as a punishment for those who don't subscribe to their "sacred" ideology. As in our *melikah* process, the neck represents obstinacy in refusal to defer to their truth. Beheading is the "smiting" or slashing of the neck of the "non-believers" as the Koran instructs. Yet, despite this parallel, our religious outlook and worldview are completely divergent from ISIS.

---

222    Rabbi Chaim Soloveitchik ruled that any nation that displays this irrational hatred towards Jews, i.e., focusing their terror and targeting the most vulnerable of our people, the aged and children, and who are willing to destroy their own lives in order to murder Jews, are halachically defined as Amalek even today.

## FLEXIBILITY AND ABILITY TO CHANGE

To us, Rosh Hashanah and really life in general is the complete antithesis. We emphasize the head because to us it embodies endless possibility. It represents using our imagination to soar upwards toward the heavens—to break the "surly bonds of Earth."[223] This may be why such prominence is given to the head of a fish as a symbol on the initial night of the festival. The fish represents procreation, productivity and expansion.[224] Our cries from the *shofar* pierce the higher realms. We are using our mouths (attached to our heads) as an expression of limit-

> WE EMPHASIZE THE HEAD BECAUSE TO US IT EMBODIES ENDLESS POSSIBILITY.

lessness, not limitation, of growth and not an untimely brutal end, particularly in the period that Hashem ponders and ultimately uses to decide our individual and communal fate.

## THE IKAR IS NOT TO FEAR

The reason we often fail at having lofty vision is something called "FEAR." We stumble, stagnate and even freeze because we don't believe in our limitless G-d-given potential. There is something beyond, a bigger picture. Marianne Williamson, in *A Return to Love,* has a popular inspirational quote:

> Our deepest fear is not that we are inadequate. Our deepest fear is that we are powerful beyond measure. It is our light, not our darkness that most frightens us. We ask ourselves, who am I to be brilliant, gorgeous, talented, fabulous? Actually, who

---

223    John Gillespie Magee, Jr. (June 9, 1922–December 11, 1941) was an American aviator and poet who died as a result of a mid-air collision over Lincolnshire during World War II. On September 3, 1941, Magee flew a high altitude (30,000 feet) test flight in a newer model of the Spitfire V. As he orbited and climbed upward, he was struck with the inspiration of a poem, "High Flight," which later became famous. It begins with the words, "Oh! I have slipped the surly bonds of Earth." See appendix 2 for the complete poem.

224    Alluded to in the famous *brachah* of Yaakov to his grandchildren, *Hamalach Hagoel,* early in *Parshas Vayechi.*

are you not to be? You are a child of G-d. Your playing small does not serve the world. There is nothing enlightened about shrinking so that other people won't feel insecure around you. We are all meant to shine, as children do. We were born to make manifest the glory of G-d that is within us. It's not just in some of us; it's in everyone. And as we let our own light shine, we unconsciously give other people permission to do the same. As we are liberated from our own fear, our presence automatically liberates others.[225]

Each of us is pure and holy, "*Elokei, neshamah she-nasata bi tehorah hi*—My Lord, the soul that you have infused me with is completely pure."[226]

The fact that we have a pure G-d-infused soul takes on an entirely new meaning each year. We must think big and realize that we can attain new levels in our spiritual aspirations. Why continue to limit and dismiss our infinite potential? Let us lift our heads proudly and imagine our better selves.

---

225    P. 190.
226    Daily prayer after *Modeh Ani.*

# A DOUBLE-EDGED SWORD

y shul, the Young Israel of the West Side, is situated next door to the Plaza Jewish Funeral Chapel.[227] For me, this juxtaposition is doubly odd. First, because I'm a *kohen*, [228] each day I have to circumvent the large awning on the street corner. Second, there's an ironic contrast between the vibrancy of a "young" shul and the quiet of the parlor next door.

THERE'S AN IRONIC CONTRAST BETWEEN THE VIBRANCY OF A "YOUNG" SHUL AND THE QUIET OF THE PARLOR NEXT DOOR.

Many times a week, I see a casket before my eyes. I often wonder to myself, how old was the person? How did they live? Did they make their mark? Once, I sensed an extra intensity on the part of the mourners on

---

227   Western corner of 91st and Amsterdam Avenue.

228   In early *Parshas Emor*, *kohanim* are restricted from coming in contact with a dead body, unless it is one of the seven close relatives.

the street. I inquired and discovered that the funeral had been for a ten-year-old boy.

## THE SHUL AND THE FUNERAL HOME

Yet the placement of my shul beside this neighbor doesn't really affect me, certainly not profoundly. I go about my business and view the funeral home "merry-go-round" as just a part of life. It is, really—except when it isn't. Except when a person's death touches me poignantly and deeply, such as after a younger person passes away, or after a spree of tragedies in Eretz Yisrael. Then I might actually take a few moments to ponder the fragility of life.

> I GO ABOUT MY BUSINESS AND VIEW THE FUNERAL HOME "MERRY-GO-ROUND" AS JUST A PART OF LIFE.

The Lubavitcher Rebbe strongly encouraged people to celebrate their Jewish birthdays, explaining that, "A birthday is the date that G-d decided that the world cannot exist without you." He taught that one should try to receive an *aliyah* to the Torah on his birthday (or on the Shabbos beforehand), and he should also give charity to the poor, and increase Torah study. Throughout his lifetime, the Rebbe marked his birthday by redoubling his efforts to reach out to Jews in every corner of the world.[229]

> "A BIRTHDAY IS THE DATE THAT G-D DECIDED THAT THE WORLD CANNOT EXIST WITHOUT YOU."

There is a comedy routine that highlights the striking shift in the way people view their birthdays as they age. "Children yearn to be grown-ups; they can't wait to get old. They even give their ages in fractions—'I'm five-and-a-half today.' Yet," the routine continues, "nobody ever says they are thirty-six-and-a-half years old."[230]

## HAPPY BIRTHDAY

Birthdays, in essence, are bittersweet; we are thankful to have reached

---

229    Reported by various people close to the Rebbe.
230    From comedian George Carlin's "Views on Aging." See appendix 3 for the complete routine.

this milestone and to have been allotted another year in this world, but at the same time a birthday is a not-so-subtle reminder to us that we are getting closer to the end. It is no wonder that many choose to ignore or hide their birthdays, or become depressed the week thereof.

IT IS NO WONDER THAT MANY CHOOSE TO IGNORE OR HIDE THEIR BIRTHDAYS, OR BECOME DEPRESSED THE WEEK THEREOF.

The passage of time is a blessing, but also an inexorable march toward death. So what do we do with this double-edged sword?

## FATE VS. DESTINY

Nearly twenty-five years ago, I attended a nighttime *levayah* in Yerushalayim. The funeral was for my friend's mother, who passed away at a young age. The officiating rabbi approached my nineteen-year-old friend as we stood in the parking lot of Har Hamenuchos after the burial, and quoted Rabbi Soloveitchik's essay *Kol Dodi Dofek*,[231] which discusses transforming "fate into destiny."

I recall being intrigued, but not grasping what these words meant. Only later did I begin to appreciate the depth of this idea, which teaches that although we can't control what happens *to* us (our fate), we can choose our reaction, which happens *through* us. In this way, we initiate our destiny—the force that shapes our fate.

---

231    *Kol Dodi Dofek* was written in 1955 as a theological response to the Shoah and the creation of the State of Israel. Its title is taken from one of the most poignant verses of the Song of Songs: "I sleep but my mind is awake. Listen! My beloved is knocking (*kol dodi dofek*). Open for me, my sister, my beloved, my dove, my perfect one." Midrashic interpretation of the Song of Songs understands it as an erotic poem about two lovers and, at the same time, as a metaphor for the relationship between G-d and his beloved Jewish people. For Rabbi Soloveitchik, it is also indicative of the existential situation that confronts the Jewish people and individual human beings alike.

Fate, in Rabbi Soloveitchik's terms, is a knocking, meant to awaken us from our slumber, challenging us to take up "man's mission in this world"; namely, to turn fate into destiny, from an existence that is passive and influenced to one that is active and influential. It is about moving from "an existence full of compulsion, perplexity and speechlessness into an existence full of will and initiative." This, according to Rabbi Soloveitchik, is the challenge posed by the Shoah and the birth of the State of Israel. These events call out to the Jewish people to move from being a passive people who let history happen to them to playing an active part in their history's unfolding.

Fate and destiny, according to Rabbi Soloveitchik, exist in dialectic, as if the two
concepts are in conversation with one another. He summarizes fate with the precept,

"MAN IS BORN AS AN
OBJECT AND DIES AS AN
OBJECT, BUT HE LIVES
AS A SUBJECT."

"Against your will you are born and against your will you shall die." The
slogan of destiny, on the other hand, is, "By your free will you shall live."
Rabbi Soloveitchik continues, "Man is born as an object and dies as an
object, but he lives as a subject."

## KADDISH OR KIDDUSH?

A few years ago, as a synagogue consultant for the Orthodox Union,
I visited a fledgling Midwestern community to provide some guidance
to the rabbi and the lay leadership. They had coined a catchy mantra to
describe the precarious state of their congregation: "*Kaddish* or *Kiddush*?"
Would their shul need a *Kaddish* recited for it, or would it be invigorated
with dynamic *Kiddushim* representing youthfulness and a vibrant future?
They decided on *Kiddush*, and were looking for ideas how to make that
happen.

"Carpe diem," the concept of seizing the day and living in the present
moment, is critical to *avodas Hashem* and
to living a healthy, balanced and productive life. I once heard that the word "fear"
is an acronym for "false evidence appearing real."[232] Fear is what happens when we
get too far ahead of ourselves and forget to focus on the present.

FEAR IS WHAT HAPPENS
WHEN WE GET TOO FAR
AHEAD OF OURSELVES AND
FORGET TO FOCUS ON THE
PRESENT.

## MOVEMENT AND FLOW

Anything living dies. Relationships end, jobs cease, communities
dwindle. The people and opportunities we once knew move on, as do
we. We die and are reborn many times on earth before we pass to the
next world, and all of these mini-death experiences are a microcosm of

---

232    Credit to my friend and corporate consultant Brent Bear for this insight.

the ultimate death experience. At each inflection point, we must gird ourselves fearlessly and tackle the present situation.

At the same time, we need to be cognizant of our own mortality, for, as we say in *Tehillim*, our days are a mere seventy years; eighty if we manage to reach "*gevuros.*" Rabbi Shlomo Wolbe strikingly writes in *Alei Shur* that from the age of thirty-five, the halfway point to seventy, we must begin to prepare ourselves for what awaits us in the next world. Elsewhere, he also says that we need to imitate the "*chassidim ha-rishonim*" by preparing daily for *tefillah*—perhaps not for an hour before and after, as they did, but at least for a minute or two.[233] We can apply this concept, as well, by occasionally reflecting on our mortality, preparing for our ultimate future. I once heard a great person say that fear of death motivated many to publish prolifically and accomplish more during their lifetimes.[234]

## A DELICATE BALANCE

This latent tension of living life while remaining aware of death echoes the delicate art of forgetting/remembering a loved one who has passed on. A *yahrtzeit*, like a birthday, is a designated special time to reflect, but it isn't meant to be perpetual. It is the same as the striking placement of a vibrant and alive "Young" Israel next door to a funeral parlor. I pass the parlor daily, but consider it only sporadically.

A mentor of mine once mentioned to me half-jokingly that he feels very comfortable and "at home" when visiting Har Hamenuchos. He remarked that this critical mindset of realizing how fleeting life is, of recognizing the interplay between fate and destiny, is more natural in the Holy Land than in the Diaspora, just as *mitzvos* are qual-

A MENTOR OF MINE ONCE MENTIONED TO ME HALF-JOKINGLY THAT HE FEELS VERY COMFORTABLE AND "AT HOME" WHEN VISITING HAR HAMENUCHOS.

---

233    In sections in *chelek beis* dealing with *vaadim* on *tefillah*, p. 348, and later in the book, dealing with *emunah* and preparation for the next world, final *maareches*, essays about what life is. I already alluded to this concept in the essay entitled "My One-Minute Speech."

234    A prominent *rav* speaking at the *levayah* of a very young man and attempting to get his friends to step up and accomplish more in their lives as they must now be a continuation of a precious life that was cut short.

itatively and quantitatively enhanced in Eretz Yisrael. In the Holy Land, it is easier to remember what life is about.

## THE END

Ultimately, death is our fate. As Benjamin Franklin said, "The only sure things in life are death and taxes." Death is real, and it is mysterious and frightening. The various statements of Chazal about death shed some light on the subject, but it still isn't easily imagined or understood.[235] As I often quip, people don't return to tell us about it.

It is our daunting task to turn our fate into our destiny, to prepare ourselves methodically for what comes next by living passionately each day while still letting go and trusting that we are in the best of hands.

The day of a person's death or *yahrtzeit* is referred to in Talmudic parlance as the "*yom hillula*," the wedding day, for that is when our souls are wedded and reunified with their Creator. Just as we prepare so meticulously for our own wedding or the wedding of a child, so must we invest in preparing for the marvelous encounter promised to us after a hundred and twenty years.

The need for this preparation should not paralyze or discourage us. We trust and believe that we only transition to our next destination when our assigned task is completed.

Every day is to be viewed simultaneously as a *zechus* and a *mechayev*. We can choose to let it pass us by, or to seize it, embrace it and use it to convert a scary fate into a glorious destiny—a destiny in which Hashem and our loved ones will be proud of our vast spiritual accomplishments.

---

235    One example is *Bava Basra* 10b speaking of an upside-down world and how people switch places from their stations and honor in this world.

# CONCLUSION

ver since my childhood, I've been an avid fan of the Dallas Cowboys football team. I watched them as a young man and can't help but follow them now even if I'm not able to watch all their games. The 2014 season ended in particularly painful fashion on a highly questionable call by the referees in a playoff game in Green Bay, Wisconsin. The head coach, Jason Garrett, a graduate of Yale University, gave a speech in the locker room postgame.

He told the story of a sixty-two-year-old man who hurt his leg when he was twenty-two and had to quit. But for forty years he would tell the story of how he hurt his leg when he was twenty-two. He told the story of a baseball player who thought he was going to be the next Sandy Koufax, but he hurt his arm and for fifty years told that story. He said, "I don't want anybody in this room to spend the rest of their lives talking about, 'But, if this ... ' Let's get out there and do what we need to do, so we have something good to talk about fifty years from now."

He made clear that what he doesn't want is a team running on empty with sadness and regret.

"There are a lot of people that we all come across," he said, "who talk about something that happened earlier in their lives—they got hurt, and a lot of their dreams and aspirations went unfulfilled. And they take those with them for the rest of their lives and refer back to that—and it's an excuse, for not achieving what they wanted to achieve.

"And so, [Sunday's] game was an opportunity for us to respond the right way to the challenges ahead and not look back and be the team that says, 'We went up to Lambeau Field and this happened and that happened,' and tell that story for forty years. We have an opportunity in front of us to learn from that experience to achieve the goals we want to achieve."

Much that happens to us is beyond our control. Curve balls and the like are par for the course of life. This book has been about cultivating an outlook and dealing with the process of responding when the chips are down. Having a broader and bigger perspective and seeing beyond ourselves are all significant in getting to wherever it is we are going. Learning from the "process" is almost as valuable as arriving at the ultimate destination.

On a personal note, I write this book at what is a little beyond the mid-point of a normal life span. I'm a work in progress and I still hold a vision of arriving at destinations I have yet to traverse. I once heard from a teacher that conceptually, "life is long," and "life isn't a race." As Rabbi Yisrael Salanter said, "If the candle still burns, there is still time to fix." If we have another day to live, then we should have faith that things can improve and we can attain different results. I'm excited about what my future holds and how this book and potentially others will play a role in that development.

Our history is important in terms of the valuable lessons it provides, but hopefully we realize it need not define our future. I hope insights in this book will help you as you move forward on your own journey and also help you in dealing with what at times can feel like an endless process.

# APPENDIX 1:
## LETTER FROM RABBI MOSHE SHAPIRO, *SHLITA*

# APPENDIX 2:
## "HIGH FLIGHT"
## BY JOHN GILLESPIE MAGEE, JR.

*Oh! I have slipped the surly bonds of Earth*
*And danced the skies on laughter-silvered wings;*
*Sunward I've climbed, and joined the tumbling mirth*
*Of sun-split clouds—and done a hundred things*
*You have not dreamed of—wheeled and soared and swung*
*High in the sunlit silence. Hov'ring there,*
*I've chased the shouting wind along, and flung*
*My eager craft through footless halls of air...*
*Up, up the long, delirious burning blue*
*I've topped the wind-swept heights with easy grace*
*Where never lark, or ever eagle flew—*
*And, while with silent, lifting mind I've trod*
*The high untrespassed sanctity of space,*
*Put out my hand, and touched the face of G-d.*

# APPENDIX 3:
## GEORGE CARLIN'S
## "VIEWS ON AGING"

o you realize that the only time in our lives when we like to get old is when we're kids? If you're less than ten years old, you're so excited about aging that you think in fractions.

"How old are you?"

"I'm four-and-a-half!"

You're never thirty-six-and-a-half. You're four-and-a-half, going on five! That's the key.

You get into your teens, now they can't hold you back. You jump to the next number, or even a few ahead.

"How old are you?"

"I'm gonna be sixteen!"

You could be thirteen, but hey, you're gonna be sixteen! And then the greatest day of your life ... you become twenty-one. Even the words sound like a ceremony... you BECOME twenty-one. YESSSS!!!

But then you turn thirty. Oooohh, what happened there? Makes you sound like bad milk! He TURNED; we had to throw him out. There's no fun now, you're just a sour-dumpling. What's wrong? What's changed?

You BECOME twenty-one, you TURN thirty, then you're PUSHING forty. Whoa! Put on the brakes, it's all slipping away. Before you know it, you REACH fifty and your dreams are gone.

But wait!!! You MAKE it to sixty. You didn't think you would!

So you BECOME twenty-one, TURN thirty, PUSH forty, REACH fifty and MAKE it to sixty.

You've built up so much speed that you HIT seventy!

After that it's a day-by-day thing; you HIT Wednesday! You get into your eighties and every day is a complete cycle; you HIT lunch; you TURN 4:30; you REACH bedtime. And it doesn't end there.

Into the nineties, you start going backwards; "I was JUST ninety-two."

Then a strange thing happens. If you make it over a hundred, you become a little kid again. "I'm a hundred-and-a-half!"

May you all make it to a healthy hundred-and-a-half!!

# ABOUT
# THE AUTHOR

Rabbi Dovid M. Cohen is a rabbi, lawyer, therapist and special-needs advocate. He has *semichah* from RIETS and also did advanced learning for a number of years in the Kollel of Yeshivas Birchas Mordechai of Beitar Ilit, an outgrowth of a popular *chaburah* in the Mir Yeshiva of Jerusalem, studying under Rabbi Yaakov Friedman and also attending *shiurim* of Rabbi Moshe Shapiro.

He holds a Juris Doctor degree from Columbia Law School and a Masters in Counseling from University of North Texas and sits as a rabbinical judge for the Beis Din of America. He is also a popular guest columnist for *Mishpacha* magazine and has a private counseling practice.

Rabbi Cohen recently completed nine years serving as Rabbi of the Young Israel of the West Side, helping to make it one of the most popular and dynamic shuls in Manhattan. He is currently Director of Synagogues for Manhattan, Bronx, Westchester and Connecticut and the Director of Community Outreach for Yachad, both roles at the Orthodox Union.

He is married to Ruchi (nee Eisenberg), daughter of the Chief Rabbi of Austria, and they live on the Upper West Side of Manhattan with their four children.

He is a coveted scholar-in-residence around the world and can be contacted for speaking engagements at cohen.dovid@gmail.com or cohend@ou.org.

# ENDORSEMENTS

Rabbi Dovid M. Cohen combines the clarity of a top attorney with the insights of a modern-day spiritual leader in this remarkable book. A must-read!

*Howard Jonas, founder of IDT Corporation and author*

Rabbi Dovid M. Cohen is one of a new breed of energetic, effective and creative rabbis who are creating a "Torah revolution" in our times. He is an insightful thinker, a stimulating speaker, and I am sure he now will prove to be a successful author as well. I look forward to more of his literary talents reaching the wider Jewish public.

*Rabbi Ron Yitzchok Eisenman, Rabbi of Congregation Ahavas Israel, Passaic, NJ,*
*Mishpacha Magazine columnist and author*

An engaging, insightful and introspective journey through the world of the pulpit rabbi and the unique prism it provides on so many of the challenges that confront us all — faith, childrearing, spirituality, marriage, joy and satisfaction. A must-read for any student of contemporary Jewish mores.

*Allen I. Fagin, Executive Vice President/*
*Chief Professional Officer of the Orthodox Union*

There are many books that address the intellect. Rabbi Dovid M. Cohen has succeeded in writing a book that also speaks to the heart. I was deeply emotionally moved, page after page. There is so much powerful inspiration for dealing with the many challenges we have to face in life; the reader will be better equipped to face them with far greater strength.

*Rabbi Jonathan Taub, senior lecturer at Machon Yaakov Yeshiva and Darchei*
*Bina Seminary and noted author*

It is a rarity to see such a young *talmid chacham*, just beginning his ascent, possessing such vast experience in so many diverse disciplines. Rabbi Dovid M. Cohen combines within his extraordinary persona the following characteristics: *rav, lamdan, posek*, guide, teacher, advisor and social worker. In this book, Rabbi Cohen brings this rich spiritual diversity to the fore as he shares with us his thoughts and his travels, with the exclusive purpose being the spreading of Torah and bringing people closer to their Father in heaven.

There is much to learn from this book as it incorporates a variety of worlds, presented in a fascinating and most uplifting fashion.

*Rabbi Yehoshua Hartman, Rosh Beis HaMedrash Hasmonean, London, and author of the multi-volume Machon Yerushalayim edition of the Maharal of Prague's works*

I have read portions of the book *We're Almost There* by Rabbi Dovid M. Cohen and found the book to contain a wealth of information from personal experiences and personal relationships with great Torah personalities. The Rabbis tell us, "There is no one wiser than one with experience." I found the material to be informative, inspiring and entertaining and recommend the book as a source for down-to-earth advice and guidance.

*Rabbi Zev Leff, Rabbi of Moshav Matityahu, Rosh Hayeshivah and Rosh Kollel of Yeshivah Gedolah Matityahu*

Wisdom is the rarest of all commodities, especially these days. But occasionally a book comes along that embodies real wisdom. Not in an overwhelming or overly intellectual way, but with simplicity, clarity, and great warmth. My dear friend and colleague Rabbi Dovid M. Cohen has produced just such a book. It is based upon his own life experiences, which makes it all the more relevant and valuable. It is engrossing because it shares dozens of precious anecdotes. It is uplifting because it discusses life's challenges and instills hope in coping with them. And it is an easy way to absorb sophisticated Torah thoughts and not even be aware of how sophisticated they are. *Kol hakavod*, Reb Dovid. You toiled in writing a book, and now you've written one, and a very good one. Please do us all a favor and write another one soon.

*Rabbi Dr. Tzvi Hersh Weinreb, Executive Vice President Emeritus of the Orthodox Union*

One of the inspiring young leaders of this generation, Rabbi Dovid M. Cohen has already impacted thousands of people and now has a broader platform to bring his wisdom to the masses.

As an accomplished attorney and a powerful rabbi, he brings a perspective that is much needed in our times. An absolute must-read!

*Paul I. Cohen, Esq., Chairman and CEO-TWC*
*Sports Management and TWC Capital Group*

Provocatively candid, profoundly inspiring, deeply moving — these will surely echo the responses of every reader of this insightful as well as highly informative new work by Rabbi Dovid M. Cohen. It is a fascinating and very personal recounting of his career in the rabbinate as well as his personal challenges marked by the birth of a special-needs child, together with his spiritual growth as he left a successful career in law to take on the difficult trials — as well as blessings — of congregational leadership. The book is a veritable window into the soul of an unusual and highly gifted contemporary spiritual leader.

*Rabbi Benjamin Blech, Professor of Talmud Yeshiva University*

Thank you, Rabbi Dovid M. Cohen for your creative insight, clarity and heartfelt writing.

*M. Gary Neuman, New York Times best-selling author*
*and creator of NeumanMethod.com.*

Rabbi Dovid M. Cohen has a remarkable ability to draw on the most private and sometimes painful personal experiences to help and guide others. Fortunate is the congregation that has such a rabbi to lead them and fortunate now are readers of this most engaging and original book.

*Yonason Rosenblum, Mishpacha Magazine and Jerusalem Post columnist*
*and founder of Jewish Media Resources*

Through his brave honesty and passionate prose, Rabbi Dovid M. Cohen has written a book which brings the reader into immediate and real engagement with the inspiring power and vital relevance of the Divine light of Torah wisdom for daily life.

*Rabbi Warren Goldstein, Chief Rabbi of South Africa*

Rabbi Dovid M. Cohen's thoughtful, inspirational and moving book provides insight and deep perspective from someone who has experienced the ups and downs in others' lives, as well as in his own.

*Gregory Zuckerman, Wall Street Journal special writer*

MOSAICA PRESS

Mosaica Press is an independent publisher of Jewish books. Our authors include some of the most profound, interesting, and entertaining thinkers and writers in the Jewish community today. There is a great demand for high-quality Jewish works dealing with issues of the day — and Mosaica Press is helping fill that need. Our books are available around the world. Please visit us at **www.mosaicapress.com** or contact us at **info@mosaicapress.com**. We will be glad to hear from you.